Black Megachurch Culture

BLACK STUDIES
& critical thinking

Rochelle Brock & Richard Greggory Johnson III
General Editors

Vol. 3

The Black Studies and Critical Thinking series
is part of the Peter Lang Education list.
Every volume is peer reviewed and meets the
highest quality standards for content and production.

PETER LANG
New York • Washington, D.C./Baltimore • Bern
Frankfurt • Berlin • Brussels • Vienna • Oxford

SANDRA L. BARNES

Black Megachurch Culture

Models for Education and Empowerment

PETER LANG
New York • Washington, D.C./Baltimore • Bern
Frankfurt • Berlin • Brussels • Vienna • Oxford

Library of Congress Cataloging-in-Publication Data

Barnes, Sandra L.
Black mega church culture: models for education and empowerment /
Sandra L. Barnes.
p. cm. — (Black studies and critical thinking; v. 3)
Includes bibliographical references and index.
1. African American churches. 2. Big churches—United States.
3. Christian sociology—United States. I. Title.
BR563.N4B378   277.30089'96073—dc22   2009049017
ISBN 978-1-4331-0909-6 (hardcover)
ISBN 978-1-4331-0908-9 (paperback)
ISSN 1947-5985

Bibliographic information published by **Die Deutsche Nationalbibliothek**.
Die Deutsche Nationalbibliothek lists this publication in the "Deutsche
Nationalbibliografie"; detailed bibliographic data is available
on the Internet at http://dnb.d-nb.de/.

FSC

Mixed Sources

Product group from well-managed
forests, controlled sources and
recycled wood or fiber

Cert no. SCS-COC-002464
www.fsc.org
©1996 Forest Stewardship Council

The paper in this book meets the guidelines for permanence and durability
of the Committee on Production Guidelines for Book Longevity
of the Council of Library Resources.

© 2010 Peter Lang Publishing, Inc., New York
29 Broadway, 18th floor, New York, NY 10006
www.peterlang.com

Printed in the United States of America

Dedicated to my grandparents, Ben Frank and Irene Barnes, who modeled the very best kind of success.

Contents

Acknowledgments

THIS RESEARCH ORIGINATES from my long-standing involvement in Black churches and my interest in how intangible factors such as belief systems and attitudes can dramatically alter people's lives. In addition to further exploring the understudied megachurch phenomenon, I was interested in focusing on the Black religious experience. Although I believe that a certain degree of mystery will always shroud how the Black community approaches religion, these findings may help to better understand long-espoused anecdotes and pre-existing notions about large Black churches and the communities they serve. In addition to using a broad methodological lens that includes quantitative and qualitative techniques, this endeavor attempts to "walk the line" between sociology and theology to consider how Black people and their God communicate in a contemporary Christian space. Because of the nature of this book, I attempted to write such that the information is accessible to a wide audience. I trust that it will be of interest to academics, clergy, theologians, laypersons interested in Black religiosity as well as readers who are simply curious about Black megachurches. Just as *seasoned* Christians proclaim that "God is good, all the time and all the time,

God is good," it was important for me to examine the beliefs, behavior, and organized efforts of churches that appear to take this sentiment literally. Hopefully this project objectively sheds additional light on some of the inner-workings, strengths, and limitations of Black megachurches.

Several groups and individuals were instrumental in bringing this book to fruition. Much thanks to the Vanderbilt University Department of Human and Organizational Development (HOD), the Louisville Institute, and a Case Western Reserve University ACES Grant for providing research support. I also appreciate both the Vanderbilt University School of Education and Divinity School for the resources and time required to complete this project. Thanks to colleagues Drs. Juan Battle of the CUNY Graduate Center, Ken Ferraro and Robert Perrucci at Purdue University, and Charlie Jaret of Georgia State University for their support. I am also grateful to my editor at Peter Lang Publishers, Dr. Rochelle Brock, and Production Supervisor, Sophie Appel, for assistance during the editorial process. I also thank Leslie Collins for reviewing an early draft of the book.

I am particularly indebted to the pastors, co-pastors, other clergy persons; as well as the administrative assistants, lay leaders, and other church officials at the Black megachurches featured in this project. Each of them was as committed as I was, in their own way, to help make this book possible. Gratitude is also in order for the leaders and members of Bethlehem Missionary Baptist Church, New Sardis Missionary Baptist Church, Clarkston First Baptist Church, First Mount Pleasant Baptist Church, Word of Life Fellowship Church, and Spruce Street Baptist Church who provided the impetus for this project. Lastly, I am profoundly grateful for the unwavering support from my extended family and friends. Particularly, my mother, Clara Brown, who continues to motivate, inspire, and challenge me to be my best and to perform academic inquiry that is culturally relative and relevant.

Introduction

THE BLACK CHURCH[1] HAS HISTORICALLY been a source of both education and empowerment in the Black community.[2] Experiences and events occurred within a specific cultural context that provided meaning and motivation for believers. Black Church cultural components such as scripture, rituals, theology, songs, and prayer informed these endeavors. For example, the bible was inspirational as well as instructional as slaves used it to learn to read. Rituals enabled Blacks to acquire social and practical skills needed to negotiate the larger society. Theology provided the wherewithal and biblical validation to face racism and classsism and live godly lifestyles despite the constant threat of social injustice. Songs and prayer undergirded community action.[3] Yet some of these same cultural tools could foster intra-church conflict as well as inequalities such as sexism and heterosexism.[4]

It has been suggested that the *Black megachurch* is the Black Church's response to modernity, secularism, and consumerism.[5] Like their predecessors, Black megachurches attempt to respond to spiritual and secular needs. Unlike their smaller counterparts, these large collectives are usually unhampered by denominationalism, traditionalism, or doctrinal constraints. In addition to size and substantial resources, I posit that Black megachurches produce, appropriate, and use culture in unconventional ways.[6] This premise brings to bear several important queries. Exactly how do Black megachurches socialize congregants to embrace a philosophy of "favor"? What traditional or nontraditional mechanisms are used to persuade congregants to believe and behave in empowered ways? What bodies of knowledge, developmental processes, or approaches foster a culture of excitement, expectation, and entitlement that convinces even the most disenfranchised persons of their worth and potential? Does the church educational process condition believers to expect things they will probably never have or is it opening their horizons for the possibility of blessings they have never imagined?

The goal of *Black Megachurch Culture* is to identify how church cultural components are created, developed, and used to educate and empower adherents and whether and how these tools are associated with the historic Black Church. I am particularly interested in how large Black congregations use symbols and rituals found in worship, theology, racial beliefs, programmatic efforts, and other tools from their cultural repertoire to instruct congregants to model success in word and deed. In addition to religious objectives, findings will illustrate that Black megachurches strive to model success on various fronts by tapping into effective historic Black Church tools and creating cultural kits that foster excitement, expectation, and entitlement. Thus salvation should be the precursor for spiritual growth and, according to some clergy, material surplus. Central to this cultural transferral is church socialization[7] processes spearheaded by charismatic senior pastors and strategically trained clergy and lay leaders. Lastly, in light of the long tradition of community service by the Black Church, this project considers how Black megachurches use varied instructional efforts to respond to education-related social problems in the Black community.

But what exactly is a *Black megachurch*? By definition, megachurches are congregations with an average attendance of 2,000 persons during weekend worship services.[8] Black megachurches have predominately Black memberships and are led by Black pastors. They also tend to include elements from the Black Church tradition during worship services. There are an estimated 120–150 Black megachurches in the United States—some dating back to the early 1900s.[9] Despite media coverage of Black megachurch pastors such as T.D. Jakes and controversial sound bites of Jeremiah Wright, few academic studies about these congregations have actually been performed.[10] In response, this project examines how Black megachurch culture is influencing the Black community in new, innovative ways. It identifies cultural tools found among a group of churches as well as how they strategically use them to educate, *re-educate*, and empower persons to expect spiritual and temporal abundance. I am interested in both traditional as well as nontraditional forms of education and instruction that comprise broader church socialization processes. When we think about education, formal institutions and events such as schools, academies, workshops, and forums typically come to mind. These organized endeavors are important and will be discussed here. However, I am equally concerned about how Black megachurches cultivate learning spaces and instructional opportunities that enable people to "think outside the box" in terms of their lives, futures, and relationships with other congregants and community members.

Although there are many avenues that could be taken when studying the Black megachurch phenomenon (i.e., political involvement, finances, and ecumenism, just to name a few), I focus attention on education-related dynamics for three primary reasons. First, educational attainment has been the primary means to upward mobility in the Black community—and the Black Church has been a central learning site. Second, detractors are stunned by the ability of Black megachurches to attract and retain throngs of supporters in a manner somewhat akin to indoctrination. Third, the ways Black megachurch pastors strategically harness the spiritual and the profane is intriguing and, I postulate, different from that of both their White megachurch and smaller Black counterparts. A unique set of circumstances appear to be cultivated in Black megachurch spaces such that *church school* is continually in session and Blacks are seeking instruction in droves.

Informed by Cultural theory,[11] quantitative and qualitative approaches,[12] and Black Church history, this book considers some of the ways Black megachurches are re-shaping the "face" of Black religiosity. I rely on the following data: in-depth interviews with clergy and survey data from 16 Black megachurches; pastoral sermons from these same congregations and 15 additional Black megachurches; and, participant observation. In order to make broader inferences about Black megachurches, I also reference national secondary data on Black small, moderately sized, and megachurches to consider how human and economic resources influence educational efforts. Given the considerable influence had by Black Church pastors, clergy interviews play a key role in explaining Black megachurch postures and programs; other data sources allow me to query "cult of personality" accusations often associated with large congregations. Broad findings based on a national sample combined with details across a specific set of Black megachurches illumine a spectrum of teaching/learning dynamics. This analysis does not represent an exhaustive study of the universe of Black megachurches, but rather provides a contextualized glimpse into the mechanisms of a cross-section of diverse congregations using the historic Black Church as a point of reference.

Education, the Black Community, and the Black Church

In *Climbing Jacob's Ladder: The Enduring Legacy of African-American Families*, Andrew Billingsley (1992) best summarizes the place of education among Blacks:

> Among all the sources of survival, achievement, and viability of African-American families, education has played a preeminent role....Education is the traditional opportunity through which Black families find their places in life. And having found it, they replicate their experience again and again through their children. (Pp. 172, 174)

For him, education has been the vehicle by which Blacks have experienced upward mobility. Working-class Black families realized that, with a college education, their children could live solidly middle-class lives; graduate degrees would help solidify socioeconomic status. This educational imperative was transferred to subsequent generations. Proponents of pathological models cannot dismiss the surplus of success stories of formally educated Blacks or national studies about the respect given education in the Black community that call into question oppositional culture theorists such as Ogbu (1978, 1991).[13] It is evident that, regardless of socioeconomic background, the majority of Blacks value education and understand its role in engendering stability and self-efficacy.[14] Many also learned from the legacy of "separate but equal" and the school of hard knocks that, despite being adaptive and resilient, in order to gain access to certain societal arenas, they needed credentials only formal education affords.

Despite the importance placed on education among Blacks, securing a quality one has been elusive to large segments of this populace historically and continues to be so today. Some camps position education as the means to reduce social disparities; others accuse this same societal institution of perpetuating them. Scholars in the Sociology of Education such as Hallinan (2001), Ravitch (2000), and Franklin et al. (1991) vividly describe how, even after public education was codified as a mainstay in the nation's movement toward meritocracy, racial segregation, discrimination, and stereotypical beliefs about ineptness meant Blacks were often barred from enrolling. Yet Black children still strove to learn in segregated, underfunded schools. However, rather than pursue a spectrum of academic subjects, Black youth and adults were usually encouraged to focus on industrial education and agrarian skills in preparation for positions in the secondary labor market.[15] Although racism was a central factor, Franklin et al. (1991) argue that fear of economic competition from Blacks prompted many Whites to bar Blacks, women, Jews, and other minorities from educational opportunities. Post-Civil War federal and state legislation did not prevent Whites, particularly in the South, from continuing to exclude Blacks from predominately White academic settings.

The early Black Church responded to segregation in a manner reminiscent of the self-help legacy forged during the invisible institution.[16] Lincoln and Mamiya (1990) describe the post-slavery response to education; "after emancipation, the newly freed people of all ages swamped the schools....Sunday schools were often the first places where Black people made contact with the educational process, first hearing, then memorizing, and finally learning to read bible stories" (p. 251). Hallinan

(2001) provides a similar comment; "Black communities tried to provide at least some access to education through the creation of Sabbath schools, night schools, and informal learning centers" (p. 51). Schools located in Black Church basements, Historically Black Colleges and Universities (HBCUs), and colleges and seminaries sponsored by Black denominations sprang up throughout the country, especially in the South. Each had a similar mission:

> All these Black schools stressed the importance of religion and moral education for the uplift of the race as it was obvious to all parties that socialization was closely tied to the educational process. The molding of young minds in the crucible of education would become determinative of the future options and economic opportunities for African Americans. (Lincoln and Mamiya 1990: 252)

Their national study on over 2,000 Black churches found that about 11 percent sponsored educational programs such as bible study, Vacation Bible school, and discussion groups and over 20 percent had programs specifically for youth. DuBois' (1903[2003]) *The Negro Church* is considered the first concerted effort to chronicle the multifaceted nature of the Black Christian experience. In addition to profiling Black religiosity and programs by denomination and location, the text is replete with references to organized fund-raising for HBCUs, denomination-specific schools, and efforts to reach the young. The book includes interviews with 1,339 Black public school children in Atlanta about their religious beliefs, church attendance, and views about the church that are impressive even for today. Other reported topics included training for ministers and candid commentary and critiques about the character and educational credentials (and sometimes, lack of) of clergy. Over nine decades later, Wilmore (1995) provides a perspective that parallels DuBois' regarding the role of education in the Black Church that also informs the current project:

> The mission of the church school can be properly pursued only where the congregation itself stresses education for all age groups and provides a total spiritual and institutional context for transformative ministries. (P. 358)

Other sources confirm this same objective: "the Black Church...encouraged education, business development, and democratic fellowship beyond its members...it represented freedom, independence...as well as the opportunity for self-esteem, self-development, leadership, and relaxation" (Billingsley 1992: 354).

Desegregation meant many Blacks no longer had to pursue an education in one-room dilapidated shacks using cast-off books—they had the legal right to attend predominately White schools. It is important to note that White schools were not *better* because Whites were better than Blacks; such schools were better because they literally had *better resources* than those found in predominately Black schools. Despite the presence of capable, caring, and committed Black teachers, Black parents knew that significant differences in school characteristics such as equipment, library books, technology, instructional resources, and the physical plant meant that, without systemic change, their children would continue to be relegated to second class status and the secondary labor market in the United States.[17] Yet education in predominately White schools was a mixed blessing. Not only do quality curricula and well-appointed learning spaces matter, but Black children need welcoming schools staffed by thoughtful, culturally sensitive administrators and instructors who promote success in all their students, regardless of race. Furthermore, instruction provided to Black children by Blacks can translate into a more positive racial and personal identity. Yet history in the United States suggests that current attempts to re-segregate school systems will turn back the clock on the possibility of equal opportunities for a quality education for children of color, especially those in poor urban locales. However, Black students who attend better-equipped, predominately White schools must often contend with a range of challenges from hostile school climates to classrooms where they are ignored or met by teachers with low expectations.[18] According to Franklin et al. (1991), despite these and many other challenges, Blacks have responded proactively because they:

> ...recognized that they must take advantage of every opportunity to make the rhetoric of democratic education a reality in their lives and in the lives of their children. (P. 50)

Continued efforts to seek a quality education have meant vigilant policing of public school systems as well as growing reliance on alternative educational institutions. Contemporary Black educators and parents are also recognizing the importance of historically segregated Black schools that, although sorely underserviced, reflected "desirable elements of African American culture worthy of maintenance and celebration" (Dempsey and Nobilt 1996: 115). Without romanticizing them, researchers such as Siddle-Walker (1996) contend that institutional caring found in *pre-Brown* Black schools addressed academic, social, and psychological needs—and that the spirit of such institutions is greatly needed today.

Whether as a result of White flight, increases in charter schools, or reduced tax bases, and despite the *No Child Left Behind* initiative, growing numbers of Black children are attending under-resourced and underserviced public schools. Many Blacks who can remove their children from public schools are doing so. Private schools sponsored by Black churches provide alternatives to inadequate public schools, secular charter schools, and potentially unwelcoming predominately White schools. Although sobering, it is clear that factors such as race, class, and neighborhood context continue to shape access to educational opportunities. Because communities—whether they are local or virtual—matter in terms of the quality of instruction, we must consider how Black megachurch communities are responding, both traditionally and nontraditionally, to the education-related dilemmas facing the Black community at large. Just as the public education system is a social structure that, at its best, can militate against inequities, it is important to assess the large Black Church as a systematized educational process designed to promote varied forms of success.

Cultural Theory

Whether it takes the form of language, food, activities, norms, or values, culture exists in every social setting. This book relies on Cultural theory to examine how culture influences Black megachurch initiatives to educate and empower people in traditional and nontraditional ways. Because of its robust applicability, I have used this paradigm in other research on the Black Church in general; it also provides an appropriate means to study Black megachurches. I describe Cultural theory here and reference it in subsequent chapters. According to Swidler (1986), culture can be defined as "symbolic vehicles of meaning, including beliefs, ritual practices, art forms, and ceremonies, as well as informal cultural practices such as language, gossip, stories, and rituals of daily life" (p. 273). This characterization deviates from previous definitions that associate culture with collective consciousness that shapes group dynamics[19] or that emphasize how ideas shape group beliefs and behavior.[20] According to this theory, culture includes socially created symbols and activities that provide meaning and help cultivate and reinforce expected behavior.[21] Using Swidler's terminology, a cultural repertoire or "tool kit" includes beliefs, symbols, stories, and rituals used to negotiate social spaces. She also contends that cultural tools are not the mechanisms by which individuals explain outcomes, but are the means to facilitate processes to bring about desired outcomes. Moreover, culture can provide both motivation *and* meaning for such processes as well as foster resource mobilization. By referencing cultural components, people are able to identify issues and problems, make sense of them, and develop responsive tactics. Swidler (1986) contends, "culture provides the materials from which individuals and groups construct strategies of action" (p. 280).

Cultural theory is referenced in this analysis to identify and describe cultural tools utilized by Black megachurches to inform, instruct, and ultimately socialize congregants to think and behave in transformative ways. Furthermore, this theoretical approach facilitates discovering: possibly new cultural tools; innovative application of existing tools; discarded tools; and, why and how "re-tooling" decisions are made. From an applied perspective, Cultural theory suggests that Black megachurch leaders would be expected to emphasize those cultural elements most apt to cultivate diverse, effective educational spaces. Like Swidler, other scholars have found connections between cultural tools and behavior in general[22] and for Black churches specifically.[23] Yet, to my knowledge, this model has not been used to study Black megachurches. Culture manifests, exists, and evolves in dynamic ways. Processing culture can institutionalize patterns to raise the consciousness

of believers, attract new supporters for a given cause, and even perme-
ate public discourse.[24] Because components of Black Church culture are
indelibly tied to group identity for some believers,[25] I consider the Black
megachurch's ability to create, control, and process culture as a pastoral-
led, yet collective endeavor—and the resulting outcomes. Furthermore,
examining the relationship between Black Church culture, meaning,
praxis, programs, and the socialization process will help broaden inquiry
on the contemporary Black religious experience.

But to what degree are the teaching and learning efforts found in
Black megachurches affected by cultural tools commonly associated
with the historic Black Church? Findings will help assess how religious
traditions are appropriated to meet individual needs and respond to systemic changes such as globalization, religious syncretism, *and* social
problems. As well as gauging their influence, it is crucial to consider the
potential strengths and limitations of cultural tools. Just as cultural components can serve as organizing agents to heighten awareness of problems and support for solutions, they may also make it difficult to alter
long-held attitudes and behavior. However, routinization may not be a
problem if, as has been suggested anecdotally, Black megachurches are
able to respond to the needs of existing members as well as proactively
develop programs and activities to proselytize and attract new ones.[26]
These types of congregational features would illustrate the benefits
associated with both the growth-seeking aspects of megachurches *and*
the "semi-involuntary" dimensions of the historic Black Church.[27]

Book Format

Some readers may be interested in Black megachurches for purely intellectual reasons; some may hope to identify best practices that can be
implemented in their organizations. Some people may be motivated by
curiosity. And still for others, considering the influence of clergy profiles,
worship, theology, and programmatic efforts may help discover innovative religious expressions that have academic and applied implications. This project attempts to capture some of the dynamic inner
workings of Black megachurches that result in a *seemingly static* model

of success. Each chapter considers a distinct aspect of Black megachurch culture that I contend either provides or cultivates education, instruction, and training. As noted earlier, it would be incorrect to consider this project a comprehensive analysis of all Black megachurches. I am interested in studying educational dynamics across a cadre of congregations. By concentrating on a finite group of education-related efforts and experiences for a finite group of congregations, I hope to detail some of the processes that both undergird Black megachurch culture and help them meet objectives. This study will also hopefully encourage inquiries on other dimensions of Black megachurch life.

Chapter 1 broadly describes demographics and general features of Black megachurches as well as connections to the historic Black Church and its cultural heritage. Although this subject has been understudied, I reference several important existing works in addition to information about the 16 Black megachurches under investigation here. Because a central focus of this book is personal empowerment and community engagement stemming from education-based initiatives, it is necessary to contextualize church efforts with descriptions of some of the most pressing challenges facing the Black community. These social problems are directly or indirectly correlated with educational parameters and thus germane to this analysis. Based on the reputation megachurches have for amassing resources and sponsoring a plethora of programs, regression modeling is used to consider how the human and economic resources associated with church size can potentially influence sponsorship of "cafeteria-style" programs in general and education and training programs in particular among Black churches.

Because I contend that education and instruction in Black megachurch settings take both traditional and nontraditional forms, Chapter 2 considers the function of worship beyond its expected celebratory purpose. Innovative worship experiences are considered a crucial proselytizing tool for megachurches; I show how worship is instructional as well. Participant observation findings and bivariate analyses help illustrate how even seemingly minor aspects of worship services can be used to inform participants about the larger church process of creating Christians who are victorious in every dimension of their lives. Chapter 3 presents some of the inner mechanisms used by church leaders to provide spiritual and practical instruction. It includes insight on subjects such as relevance, leadership training, succession, and collaborative processes with other secular institutions. Of equal consequence during church socialization processes are instances when teaching and learning go awry and how church leaders adapt and respond. I also document more traditional educational methods such as Day Schools, Christian academies, and GED programs.

Although this work does not examine the full range of theologies espoused by the sample churches, in-depth interviews, sermon data, and direct observations are referenced in Chapter 4 to compare and contrast use of Black and Womanist Liberation theologies. Initially espoused by the Black religious intelligentsia, these theologies have been associated with self-actualization, social consciousness, and the fight for social justice. I question whether and how messages of liberation are evident in the posture and plans of Black megachurches, appropriated in unexpected ways, and extended to congregational behavior. It is also important to consider these more prophetic perspectives because existing research ascribes a conservative theology to megachurches. Clergy thoughts on the subject are augmented by regression modeling to illustrate how Liberation theologies can affect church educational programs.

In Chapter 5, each of the sample churches is profiled with emphasis on their educational efforts. The applied nature of the chapter enables readers to compare and contrast Black megachurch programs with those of their respective congregations, secular organizations, and Black churches in general. In addition to best practices, it considers an array of activities that challenge our understanding of what it means to educate and instruct. In light of the Black Church history of community action and social challenges in the Black community, the chapter closes with a typology of short- and long-term educational programs based on benevolence and social justice. Complaints continue about the subpar nature of public educational systems, especially in poor communities of color. I conclude the book with observations and assessments about some of the spiritual and secular dynamics predicted to influence future programmatic efforts among Black megachurches as well as how these churches will continue to impinge upon societies' expectations about acceptable religious spaces.

Notes

1. The "invisible institution" refers to the informal meetings of Blacks during and post-slavery before the formal Black Church was organized. Throughout this book, "Black Church" refers to the collective institution and "Black church" refers to individual congregations. Use of the former term should not suggest to readers the lack of diversity among Black congregations (even Black megachurches) based on factors such as denomination, theological focus, worship style, programmatic efforts, and community involvement. In addition, elements that suggest a unique "Black flavor" in the Black Church tradition are formally known as Black Church culture and are discussed in subsequent chapters (Billingsley 1999; Costen 1993; Lincoln and Mamiya 1990; Wilmore 1995). For the sake of consistency, the term "Black" is used to refer to "African Americans."

2. Billingsley (1999), Felder (1991), Lincoln (1984), Lincoln and Mamiya (1990), Mays and Nicholson (1933).

3. Barnes (2004, 2005), Carter (1976), Lincoln and Mamiya (1990), Morris (1984), Pattillo-McCoy (1999), Wilmore (1994, 1995).

4. Barnes (2006), Collins (2000), Dyson (1996), Gilkes (2001), Lincoln and Mamiya (1990).

5. Hartford Institute of Religious Research (2005), Lee (2005), Tucker (2002), Tucker-Worgs (2002).

6. Harrison (2005), Lee (2005, 2007), Thumma and Travis (2007), Tucker (2002).

7. Socialization is commonly defined as the process by which persons come to understand themselves, society, how society views them, and ways to reach their goals and objectives in life. The same concept can be applied to organizational processes where groups attempt to instruct adherents about how to be appropriate members by conveying norms, values, expectations, and behavior.

8. Hartford Institute of Religious Research (2005), Tucker (2002), Tucker-Worgs (2002).

9. Dart (1991), Hartford Institute of Religious Research (2005), Thumma and Travis (2007), Tucker-Worgs (2002). Most megachurches have higher average attendance. In literature, the terms "megachurch" and "mega church" are used interchangeably. The use of "weekend" rather than just Sunday as the selection criterion is based on the tendency for some megachurches to also sponsor worship services on Saturdays. Schaller (2000) suggests a similar definition, but includes church features other than size and thus moves beyond a dichotomous definition. Although they comprise less than one percent of all congregations, megachurches have an estimated 4 million weekly attendees. Megachurches represent the largest 10 percent of U.S. congregations and account for about half of all churchgoers (Chaves 2004; Ellingson 2007; Schaller 2000; Vaugh 1993). Thumma and Travis (2007) estimate about 1,250 Protestant megachurches in the United States.

10. Dart (1990), Lee (2005, 2007), Tucker (2002), Tucker-Worgs (2002). To my knowledge, the latter researcher's dissertation is the most detailed examination of Black

megachurches to date.

11. Benford (1993), Swidler (1986, 1995).

12. Approaches include content analysis and regression modeling, respectively. The latter is a common quantitative approach used here to test Black Church dynamics using a national data file. Content analysis is a qualitative method used to identify: meanings in the data; common, emergent themes; and, response patterns often overlooked by other techniques (Denzin and Lincoln 2005; Krippendorf 1980). This approach was used to analyze the interview and sermon data. Direct observation data also augment the interview findings.

13. Refer to the groundbreaking article by Ainsworth-Darnell and Downey (1998).

14. Ainsworth-Darnell and Downey (1998), Matthews-Armstead (2002).

15. Morris (2004), Ravitch (2000).

16. Refer to DuBois (1903[2003]), Dyson (1996), Higginbotham (1993), and, Lincoln and Mamiya (1990).

17. Ibid.

18. Hallinan (2001), Ravitch (2000).

19. Consider Durkheim's (1964) historic work.

20. Weber (1930, 1946) provides another classical assessment of this concept.

21. Swidler (1986).

22. Bellah et al. (1996), Bourdieu (1977, 1984), Goffman (1974).

23. Drake (1940), McRoberts (2003), Pattillo-McCoy (1999), West (1982), Wilmore (1994).

24. Swidler (1995).

25. Costen (1993, 1995), Drake (1940), Gallup and Castelli (1989), Taylor (1988), Wilmore (1994).

26. Ellingson (2007), Thumma and Travis (2007).

27. Ibid., Ellison and Sherkat (1995), Harrison (2005), Lincoln and Mamiya (1990), McRoberts (1999), Sherkat and Ellison (1991).

Chapter One

The Black Megachurch Phenomenon

Influences, Challenges, and Responses

About Black Megachurches

Before examining specific profiles and programs, I present a general portrait of Black megachurches. This section is informed by the extant, albeit limited, scholarship by Harrison (2005), Lee (2005), Schaller (2000), Thumma and Travis (2007), and Tucker (2002) who have investigated megachurches in general or Black megachurches in particular. The general consensus is that an increasing number of Blacks are joining megachurches. Approximately 6.7 percent of megachurches have over 50 percent Black adult participants; about 10.5 percent of megachurch attendees are Black. Moreover, estimates suggest that 10–12 percent of megachurches today are Black megachurches.[1] In addition to descriptions provided in the introductory chapter, common features of large Black congregations include: Black, charismatic senior pastors;[2] multiple, energetic, hi-tech weekend worship services; televised broadcasts; and, cafeteria-style programs. Black megachurches also tend to be independent congregations or affiliated with self-governing denominations such as Baptists.

Like the congregations sampled here, organizationally, such church-es maintain large paid and volunteer staffs, emphasize small group involvement, and hold high expectations for membership commitment and proselytizing.[3] As suggested by a representative quote from a pas-tor of a Baptist church in the Washington, D.C., area profiled in this study, the significant growth among Black megachurches is tied to the latter dynamic; "evangelical...we believe in an aggressive evangelistic outreach ministry." Furthermore, large edifices, satellite locations, and, enterprises such as bookstores, community development corporations (CDCs), and schools are common.[4] Scholarship posits that those clergy that best understand the current religious "marketplace" have posi-tioned their congregations for substantial growth. For example, Schaller (1990) presents 24 reasons for the megachurch explosion in which the most attractive congregations are able to: make church going relevant; provide motivational preaching; and, sponsor multifaceted programs that meet religious and personal needs. It is not surprising to those who study the Black religious experience that the above variables that asso-ciate the growth of the church to "Adam Smith's marketplace" (Niebuhr 1995: 1), when combined with historic church participation trends among Blacks, would result in substantial Black megachurch expan-sion. Yet heterogeneity can be found across large Black congregations. Just as they reflect dimensions from their Black Church predecessor, they also reflect vestiges from White Evangelical Protestantism, the larger society, and cultural tools of their own making.

It goes without saying that decision-making is affected by church location. Land acquisition and usage have been considered a point of contention between megachurches and local municipalities where megachurch growth largely means expansion into suburban hinter-lands. Thumma and Travis (2007) attempt to dispel the myth that megachurches are generally land guzzlers and natural resource hogs that provide little real benefit to the areas to which they migrate. I contend that an even stronger argument can be made for the community-relat-ed benefits wrought by Black megachurches, particularly for urban con-gregations known for refurbishing blighted properties or churches that migrate to predominately Black suburban spaces experiencing White flight. It would be safer to wager that conflict about *Black megachurch* land usage would largely arise when these congregations choose to venture into predominantly White suburban spaces. Nonetheless, Black megachurches are equally likely to be located in urban or suburban communities and disproportionately represented in states such as Georgia, Texas, and Florida. Among the 16 Black megachurches examined here, approximately 53 percent ($n = 8$) are located in urban areas, 40 percent (6) are suburban, and one (7 percent) is a rural church. Although several churches exceed 25,000 members, the average membership size is slightly over 8,000 persons.

In their seminal analysis on Black religiosity, *The Black Church in the African-American Experience,* Lincoln and Mamiya (1990) predicted that better-educated Blacks would increasingly require their churches to provide more informed, thoughtful, and relevant preaching and programs. On the basis of the Black megachurches profiled in this study, membership and ministry are just as diverse as the profiles of the clergy that serve them. For example, 12 of the Black megachurches (80 percent) can be considered class diverse with membership mixes across the socioeconomic spectrum. However, two congregations have largely middle- and upper-class memberships and two congregations are predominately working class and poor. A review of pastors' profiles confirms Niebuhr's (1995) assertions that "some of the fastest growing [megachurches]…are predominately Black, spiritual homes to congregations run by ministers skilled in both preaching and management" (p. 1). All of this study's pastors are full-time clergy and thirteen (81 percent) have earned at least a Doctor of Ministry degree. Indicative of the political inclinations among historic Black churches, five pastors are or have been formally involved in politics—two as senators, one as a congressperson, another, as a long-time delegate, and one as a superdelegate during the 2008 presidential election. Niebuhr (1995a) also provides an assessment germane to these types of Black megachurch leadership profiles:[5]

> Many if not most megachurches were led by "extraordinarily talented pastor-entrepreneurs. These are men who, if they had gone into business, would have been CEOs…if they had gone into politics, they would have been senators." (P. 3)

The members of the Black megachurch expect *more* from their home congregations in terms of worship, preaching, teaching, activities, and programs. It has been suggested that one of the strengths or draws of large congregations is their ability to sponsor a variety of ministries and programs. As suggested by the following observation, these cafeteria-style programs—often offered 24 hours a day, 7 days a week— are enticing, particularly to under-serviced Black urban communities:

> Megachurches have mega programs. Black churches have always emphasized social services. Now the growing number of predominately African-American megachurches are aggressively expanding outreach and economic develop- ment efforts in ways that are transforming entire communities. (ReligionLink: "Black megachurches' Mega-Outreach" 2004)

Niche programs and cell groups attempt to address secular and spiritu- al needs of congregants and residents in surrounding spaces. Such efforts also help retain members and attract new ones where people from the latter group are drawn to needed programs, practical preaching, and uplifting praise. It can also be argued that Christians have come to expect more from their local churches because people have come to expect more from society in general. According to Schaller (2000), "con- sumerism has changed the rules of the game" (p. 17) and created an envi- ronment ripe for the growth of large congregations because people now have high expectations from churches and desire "one stop shopping" (p. 58) to meet their sundry religious needs and proclivities. Churches that have strategically responded to consumerism have experienced growth. Some Black Christian *consumers* have spiritual and temporal needs that they believe are not addressed in large White churches or smaller Black ones—these persons are often attracted to Black megachurches.[6] For educated, middle- and upper-class Blacks as well as their less economically stable counterparts with similar interests who want a more cathartic religious experience *and* dynamic, practical pro- grams, Black megachurches represent a formalized agent to meet these requirements. In addition to providing tangible responses to needs, I contend that Black megachurches *model* expected success for a diverse populace—despite negative social forces—and endeavor to create spaces to equip persons to experience success in every facet of their lives.

The Contemporary Black Church and Its Predecessor

It is well known that the Black Church is one of the oldest organizations in the Black community and one of few institutions owned and controlled by Blacks.[7] The historic Black Church reflected an amalgamation of cultural components from the African and U.S. traditions shaped in response to systemic constraints such as slavery, segregation, and discrimination. But to consider the institution largely a response to negative interactions with White society undermines the agency of early leaders such as Lemuel Haynes, George Liele, Richard Allen, Absalom Jones[8] and countless unknown persons who sought to establish places of worship more germane to the legacy and everyday experiences of Blacks. Self-governing Black congregations represented racially independent spaces for worship and praise. They also reflected environments for organized efforts to counter White supremacy and systematically resocialize Blacks to think differently about themselves, their communities, and their potential. Extensive studies corroborate the Black Church's multifaceted dimensions.[9] In addition to providing a safe haven from discriminatory practices, the Black Church: helped adherents develop healthy racial identities; served as an arena for wholesome cultural, educational, and social activities; was the seat of Black-led activism and self-help initiatives; and, created a domain where political leaders and volunteers could be recruited and developed. Of equal import, it served as tangible evidence that Blacks had the fortitude, savvy, and know-how to establish and maintain institutions outside the purview and control of Whites.

When DuBois (1903[2003]) documented Black religious life in the early 1900s, he estimated approximately 23,463 Black churches in the United States; today, this number has more than tripled. In addition to continued representation among the African Methodist Episcopal (AME), African Methodist Episcopal Zion (AMEZ), Baptist, Christian Methodist Episcopal (CME), Church of God in Christ (COGIC), Presbyterian, and United Methodist denominations, a growing number of Black churches are nondenominational. These latter congregations can retain the organizational benefits of traditional denominations without the bureaucracy or national accountability. In addition, Black churches must now compete with non-Black congregations as well as parareligious organizations for the time, talents, and financial support of Blacks.[10] Despite the competitive nature of contemporary religious spaces, Black megachurches appear to have emerged above the fray as nuanced representations of the historic Black Church and heterogeneity found in the Black community.

What of the contemporary Black Church and its variations? What can we learn by comparing and contrasting their demographic and programmatic profiles? Table 1.1 provides broad church and clergy profiles for a national sample of Black churches that allows for comparisons with the 16 churches investigated in this project.[11] The table includes separate categories that identify Black smaller, moderately sized, and megachurches from the national data followed by the current purposive sample. Church size is defined as average attendance during Sunday worship services. Readers who study congregational life or who are active in a church know that rolls are notoriously overinflated with inactive members. Thus average Sunday attendance is believed to more accurately represent church size and member involvement. Furthermore, scholars such as Schaller (1990) suggest that megachurches are often more concerned about attendance than membership. Fourteen of the churches from the national sample can be considered Black megachurches based on their average Sunday worship attendance of at least 2,000 persons. Additionally, because the definition in this secondary data source only considers Sunday worship, it is quite possible that some of the largest churches in the second category would, in fact, be considered megachurches if the variable captured weekend worship services.

The majority of Black megachurches in both the national and purposive samples are affiliated with the Baptist tradition and located in urban spaces. A greater relative percentage of pastors from larger Black churches are formally trained and hold full-time positions at their respective congregations. Paralleling earlier research on megachurches, practical sermons and proactive efforts to assimilate new members are more common as church size increases.[12] Other indicators typically associated with Black Church cultural tools are meaningful, including more frequent sermonic references to spirituality and a social justice focus, but relatively less emphasis on Liberation theologies.[13] The tradition of educational efforts is apparent across the two databases as congregations offer a wide array of teaching and learning opportunities.[14] For example, regardless of church size, over 94 percent of congregations sponsor religious education classes such as bible studies beyond Sunday school. Similarly, at least 93 percent also offer prayer/meditation groups. These figures are markedly different from those found by Thumma and Travis (2007) for megachurches in general. For example, in their analysis, 66 and 71 percent of megachurches, respectively, report that religious education classes or prayer/meditation groups are key church activities. As illustrated in Table 1.1, a greater relative percentage of larger Black churches in general sponsor more and varied programs as compared to their smaller and moderately sized counterparts. This suggests that, as church size increases (as evidenced by Sunday worship attendance), so does the presence of the types of education programs highlighted here. Furthermore, the vast majority of the 16 Black megachurches profiled in this current project sponsor such programs. The statistics presented in Table 1.1 represent some of the more current program patterns for Black churches. They also provide a preview of some of the efforts described latter in this book. Although one might concede that Black megachurch programs are impressive, detractors argue that they are woefully inadequate when compared to the types of social problems facing the Black population and the resources available to large congregations.

Black Community Challenges

Despite Black Church educational programs, Blacks, especially the poor, continue to experience hardships directly or indirectly related to educational attainment that undermine their upward mobility and quality of life. Literature on social capital reminds us about the relationship between formal education and many of the social problems in the Black community. This section provides a summary of systemic and individual challenges associated with poverty, subpar public educational systems, health issues, and wealth inequities and how the Black megachurches in this study are responding. In light of the thrust of this book, I do not attempt to present all of the social problems confronting the Black populace, but rather profile some of the most pressing conditions that have been correlated with educational attainment or the lack thereof.

In the United States, socioeconomic status is intimately associated with educational attainment. This means that, in the Black community, *the least of these* are typically impoverished *and* un- or undereducated. For example, although Blacks comprise about 14 percent of the U.S. population,[15] they are disproportionately represented among the poor. In 2006, poverty rates by race/ethnicity were 24.3 percent for Blacks, 20.6 percent for Hispanics, 10.3 percent for Asians, and 8.2 percent for non-Hispanic Whites. About 60 percent of poor Black children live at or below poverty.[16] Minimally, poverty means that people are often without the basic necessities to survive. In response, each congregation in this study provides food programs and cash outlays. In addition to internally driven subsistence programs, the sample Black megachurches are likely to offer assistance via alliances with community agencies, grocery stores, food banks, and referrals. For those located in food deserts, efforts to combat poverty are typically large in scope, extensive, creative, and well organized:

> All of our programs are at least 25 years old. The food bank started just as a normal food give away and I prayed and asked the Lord to give us a building. I wanted something like 7–11. And now our food bank is set up where people can take a grocery cart, walk through, get cans from the shelves, get bakery items…there's a system set up. (pastor of a Holiness church in the Washington, D.C., area)

According to the pastor whose views are given in the extract above, God enabled his church to substantially expand a stock benevolence ministry such that it parallels a traditional grocery store. Intentionally creating a traditional shopping *experience* means persons feel "normal" as they receive assistance. Similarly, the pastor of a Midwestern church affiliated with the United Church of Christ (UCC) describes both internal services and secular alliances established to combat hunger:

> We have Food Share which is once a month people can come and get a food basket. We have constant walk-ins; we have coupons to the local Jewel store separate and distinct from the Food Share. At Thanksgiving, we give away full

baskets that include a turkey—just about 2,000 every Thanksgiving. And Christmas Day, we bring in women from the shelter and their children and feed them from the church. Cash assistance…we're talking about a quarter of a million dollars a year give away cash assistance. We have a limit in terms of how high it can go and how many times you can get it. Normally because the demand was so high, we put a $650 limit on it…sometimes we have to bury somebody.

Church location in an impoverished urban space means that local residents are often church members. This church's organized "cradle to grave" ministry format is well known in the city and community. For the pastor, part of effectively responding to social challenges such as hunger requires short-term solutions as well as long-term strategies correlated with education, training, and gainful employment. Similarly, a clergy representative from a Baptist church in Atlanta, Georgia, contends that economic benevolence combined with educational training is needed to experience upward mobility:

> Our Needs Empowerment ministry…we call it the empowerment ministry because members come to the church with a financial need, but then we empower you so that you're able to take control of your finances to move forward…our entrepreneurial training school is bursting at the seams…the word is getting out that you can equip yourself to move forward.

The pastor of a Holiness church in Washington, D.C., has intentionally remained in a poor urban area to revitalize it. One of the church's many programs is a clothing bank. However, unlike typical ministries that provide clothes, it sponsors a boutique where people are provided with vouchers to purchase items. Only dry-cleaned items can be donated. All items are gently used; many are upscale and designer clothes. And *shoppers* place their desired items in shopping carts. Furthermore, the facility is decorated to resemble a boutique to make the shopping experience as *normal* as possible. Thus those in need are able to get free, often namebrand attire in a comfortable, attractive environment that does not focus on their impoverished status. Similarly, a Baptist church in Atlanta, Georgia, sponsors extensive job training and employment placement workshops and programs. In addition to training participants to develop resumes, successfully interview, and locate gainful employment, the program helps people learn how to dress for success—and provides them with appropriate attire.

In both these examples, Black megachurches are attempting to simultaneously respond to structural forces, in these instances, poverty and employment dynamics, and expand the scope of choices available to the economically challenged. Akin to Maslow's hierarchy of needs, clergy believe that their churches must address short-term needs such as food, clothing, and shelter before responding to more long-term challenges such as education and training. And efforts that help meet basic human needs position and prepare recipients to avail themselves of other church programs designed to help them become self-sufficient. It is common that assistance programs also instill a sense of appreciation and commitment among recipients to the sponsoring congregation and its efforts—stimulating church attendance and membership. For practical reasons, church-sponsored clothing outlets help the working poor negotiate society without calling attention to their socioeconomic status. Sociopsychologically, attire can affect attitude and, according to these clergy, *aptitude*, if recipients begin to view themselves more favorably and think and behave accordingly. Similarly, access to quality foodstuffs that are not merely grocery store or restaurant castoffs can provide more than sustenance, but help feed the *spirits* of the poor. And in doing so, clergy contend that the less fortunate are more prone to develop spiritually, mentally, and *aesthetically*, in part, to formal instruction, but also by example.

In *The Hidden Cost of Being African American,* Shapiro (2004) describes examples of generational advantage due to ascription that middle- and upper-class Whites experience through inheritances, family gifts, and subsidized college education. In contrast, even middle-class, college-educated Blacks who live frugally tend to be "asset poor" and lack the requisite capital to lessen the wealth gap between themselves and their White middle-class peers. Poor Blacks lag even further behind. As noted earlier, the vast majority of the sample Black megachurches are class mixed. This heterogeneity provides a space where more economically stable Blacks are expected to help empower their economically challenged counterparts based on an overall church edict to serve:

We have a lot of folks in the church who are professionals and they are very generous with their expertise. We help people directly with access to funds and then indirectly with information that will help them to live their life or break out of poverty...as folks tithe to us 10 percent of their income, we tithe it right back out...all of that has to be a sense of how the church's theology or its biblical understanding is rooted. I think if you have a Matthew 25 or an Acts 1 view of the world, you'll do something like that. (pastor of a Baptist church in Washington, D.C.)

A Social Gospel message informs the above church's programs and community outreach. In addition to collective tithing efforts, part of the pastor's mission is to also encourage middle- and upper-class congregants to tithe their individual resources and social capital. In doing so, the formally educated become volunteer instructors for the less educated during church-sanctioned, church-sponsored courses, bible studies, forums, and workshops. As they acquire expertise and social capital, the latter group members are able to take on instructive roles. In this way, activities take place in spiritually "safe spaces" by organizations reputed for providing services in nonpaternalistic ways. This pastor's philosophy does not imply that poor people initially have little of value to offer or that they are relegated to the status of recipients from their well-off church peers, but reflects the stark reality that, relative to formal education, his economically challenged members can benefit from the social capital of their counterparts.

In a credentialed society, gatekeeping is common in employment arenas; formal education is expected and rewarded. According to C. Wright Mills (1956), such training is believed to be central for personal advancement. Yet 2003 literacy figures show that about 24 percent of Blacks lacked basic literacy skills as compared to 7 and 14 percent of Whites and Asians, respectively. A sample pastor of a Baptist church in an urban locale corroborates these trends: "one of the consequences of poverty is illiteracy." Whether or not one agrees with his causal ordering, according to 2005 census figures, 80 percent of Blacks aged 25 years or older had at least a high school diploma; yet only 17 percent of this same group had earned at least a bachelor's degree.[17] Furthermore, college retention rates for Black students are variable. For example, 2006 statistics from the *Journal of Blacks in Higher Education* show that the national college graduation rate for Black students was 43 percent, a dramatic increase from 2003 statistics, yet still significantly below the White rate of 63 percent.[18] These comparative rates by race are important because Blacks who earn a college degree have a median income near parity with similarly educated Whites. Yet, as a group, Blacks, especially the poor, continue to lag substantially behind Whites.[19] Given these types of challenges, 50 percent of the sample Black megachurches sponsor Day Schools or private academies; adult education programs are also the norm (formal educational programs are discussed further in Chapter 3). These institutions provide traditional education, but also enable congregations to systematically and formally communicate their specific theologies. As noted by the pastor of a Baptist church in the Washington, D.C., area, sponsoring schools also helps build relationships between churches and families who avail themselves of these services:

> This is really an avenue for reaching out into the community. And so it touches people through the voucher program, people who would not be able, under normal circumstances, to afford private education....So we're dealing with the impoverished as a means of affecting their lives long term.

The above congregation also sponsors an adult literacy program through a secular alliance. Driven by the pastor's entrepreneurial experiences, the next church's efforts include an employment ministry, traditional financial support, budgeting classes, and housing aid. Goals vary, but include helping people escape poverty, locate gainful employment, become more economically stable—and ultimately build generational wealth:

> We have job fairs at least once a quarter and oftentimes more than that...when we financially assist a member we try to get them plugged in, not to just getting a check from [church name], but also, let's get you into our budgeting class so...they're able to see the issues that led to them needing financial assistance and then hopefully how to avoid the situation in the future. (clergy representative from a Baptist church in Atlanta, Georgia)

Biblical healings of sickness are miraculous encounters with the nebulous and fantastic. However, the existence and effects of health inequities on the Black community are all too real. Health disparities are directly correlated with systemic inequality. Yet individual decision-making affects the prevalence of chronic, generally preventable conditions such as high blood pressure, diabetes, and human immunodeficiency virus (HIV). Members of the Black community are more likely to have higher rates of untreated illnesses and experience such conditions.[20] Moreover, dynamics such as environmental racism, substandard housing, stress, and poor diet among growing numbers of Blacks are only exacerbated by the absence of or limited, affordable healthcare. For example, although 2006 health insurance statistics remained statistically unchanged for Whites (10.8 percent are without coverage), figures increased for Blacks from 2005 to 2006 from 19.0 to 20.5 percent.[21] Additionally, studies consistently show that HIV/AIDS disproportionately impacts the Black community. According to 2005 Centers for Disease Control figures, 33 percent of all cumulative AIDS cases as well as the majority of new AIDS cases in the United States are Black.[22] The above health statistics are sobering and even more staggering as they play out in the daily lives of *real* people. Nor do they do justice to psychological and emotional maladies not detailed in this analysis that challenge the Black populace, particularly those too poor to get sick.[23]

A group of Black megachurches in this study is attempting to respond to health challenges by focusing on education-based preventions and interventions. The following representative quote from a pastor of a Baptist church in the Midwest underscores their efforts:

> We're providing all kinds of health forums and health fairs throughout the community...we're already providing psychological services. We also have on our ministerial staff a PhD in psychology.

Like this clergy, congregations here that sponsor health programs rely on multi-pronged responses that tap into church and community resources where the particular Black megachurch stands as the architect of the process. When HIV/AIDS is specifically mentioned, the following clergy representative from a Disciples of Christ church located in Atlanta, Georgia, has responded through intra-church education, secular alliances, and community outreach:

> Because of the prevalence of new HIV cases identified in the African American community, we want to look at ways to sensitize our members, not only education, but service....Our church makes concerted efforts to partner with other

agencies…efforts to involve the faith community in addressing poverty and HIV/AIDS and other social issues in our community.

Most clergy here are not naïve about the challenges facing growing segments of the Black community. In the spirit of the Black Church self-help tradition, they position their churches to respond accordingly. Yet informed by this same tradition, churches are also emboldened to tap into secular tools and networks to accomplish their objectives.

Specific church programs and belief systems that shape them are described in subsequent chapters. However, one general observation evident among the sample clergy should be noted at this juncture. Regardless of clergy and church profile, the sample Black megachurches are most likely to offer ministries and programs in response to social problems that affect a disproportionate percentage of Blacks. Like their religious predecessors, they describe efforts to combat economic, social, and political inequalities and injustices. And these Black megachurches appear to be *proactive* in their work to combat challenges associated with poverty, housing issues, health issues, incarceration rates, single parent families, and employment inequities through, among other methods, education-related initiatives.

Most programs reflect the historic Black Church self-help tradition and a linked fate mentality, but based on church resources and missions, tend to be significantly larger in scope. For example, each of the 16 profiled congregations sponsors community service programs. Similarly, all of the churches believe they are working a great deal for social justice. The expected cafeteria-style program format is also evident; approximately 80 percent (12) of the congregations sponsor forty or more programs or ministries.[24] The following pastor of a Holiness church in the Washington, D.C., area paraphrases 3 John 1:2 to explain why Christian ministry should encompass a multitude of concerns and needs:

> I believe God wants us to have wealth. He wants us to prosper, but He also says He wants us to be in health as our soul prospers…take care of the whole man, the whole physical man.

Reflecting belief in the well-known anecdote that people "do better" when they "know better," congregations here promote a varied approach when responding to social problems. They realize that effective educational efforts must be imbedded within a broader programmatic system that first meets basic needs. Simply put, clergy concede that it will be difficult for people to strive to improve spiritually, intellectually, emotionally, and culturally if they are hungry, sick, naked, or homeless. Such Maslovian beliefs may parallel those found in smaller Black churches and White megachurches. However, results from this analysis illustrate how the twofold nature of what it ostensibly means to be "Black" and "mega" often result in agendas that differ dramatically from those found in the latter two religious groups.

Does Size Matter?

The term "cafeteria-style programs" arises in literature on outreach and in-reach efforts of megachurches. The term refers to the tendency of large churches to sponsor numerous and diverse programs both in response to membership needs and desires as well as in anticipation of them. The concept conjures up images of a smorgasbord where your every culinary delight can be satisfied. It further suggests that savvy churches are becoming much more empathetic and proactive to meet the multiple concerns of congregants and potentially attract new members. Scholars such as Tucker (2002), Thumma and Travis (2007), and Lee (2005) write of different megachurch offerings, but also allude to growing concerns by detractors that, given their considerable human, economic, and political resources, megachurches are not doing all they can. Those most critical suggest that too many megachurches are more concerned with large congregations, large campuses, and large coffers than they are about using their resources to intervene on behalf of the less fortunate. Because of their size, megachurches cannot hide. And to whom much is given, much is *expected*. But just as size matters to onlookers, how do substantial resources actually play out for large *Black* congregations? Niebuhr (1995a) describes the cycle as follows:

> Fast-growing churches enter a cycle: More people coming through the doors means more money in the collection plate, which goes to more programs, some of which are charitable; a larger staff, even a bigger building. All of this in turn draws more people. (P. 1)

So as a church grows, the number and types of needs of its members would be expected to grow. Similarly, having more members generally means that a church has additional human and economic resources to sponsor more programs. Although previous case studies broadly describe the types of programs and/or ministries some Black megachurches provide, to my knowledge, no researcher has statistically identified the types of church features, including size, that tend to foster "cafeteria-style" programs.

Using the national data referenced earlier, I rely on modeling to answer the following two broad questions:[25] What types of Black churches tend to sponsor a large and varied number of programs? Next, as anecdotally described in earlier research, do larger churches tend to offer cafeteria-style programs more so than their smaller counterparts? In these tests, I continue to use average Sunday worship attendance (ranging from 0 to 3,500 or more persons) to capture church size.[26] The definition of cafeteria-style programs includes a total of 23 religious and practical programs such as bible study, youth programs, singles programs, spiritual retreats, computer literacy, social advocacy programs, food banks, and clothing programs (the entire list of programs as well as details about modeling, data strengths and limitations, and variable definitions are provided in the appendix). As will be illustrated in Chapter 5, this list does not attempt to include the plethora of programs offered by the churches in this study (or other churches as well), but rather reflects a broad inventory of church offerings discussed or studied in academic research on Black religiosity and available in this secondary data source.

Table 1.2 summarizes results from a series of linear regression models that assess the influence of church size and other church and clergy demographics on program sponsorship (actual model output is provided in the appendix). By examining trends found among a group of small, moderately sized, and megachurches, I can determine some of the indicators that help identify the types of Black congregations that sponsor cafeteria-style programs. If "church size" matters, larger congregations would be expected to sponsor more and varied programs. Five distinct models are developed. Each one includes the variables from the previous test(s) as well as additional indictors studies suggest reflect megachurch features. I focus on nine indicators: (1) church size, (2) denomination (Baptist versus non-Baptist), (3) urban location, (4) pastor's education, (5) pastor's paid status, (6 and 7) sermon types (practical or spiritual focused), (8) whether the church has a social justice focus, and (9) church efforts to assimilate new members. These are not the only possible variables that could be considered nor do the outcomes reflect the efforts of the population of Black megachurches. However, the results illustrate how church size can influence the type and number of programs Black congregations sponsor even after other dynamics have been considered.

When denominational difference is assessed alone in Model 1, Baptist churches tend to sponsor cafeteria-style programs as compared to their non-Baptist counterparts. However, considering church size in Model 2 renders denominational effects insignificant. Two points are noteworthy. First, as expected, as church size increases, so do the number of programs they sponsor—the largest Black churches (a group that includes Black megachurches) tend to offer more and varied programs than smaller or moderately sized Black churches. Second, church size is a more important predictor of extensive program sponsorship than denomination. In Model 3, church size continues to be important. Moreover, Black churches that are located in urban areas tend to sponsor more cafeteria-style programs than those in nonurban (i.e., suburban and rural) areas. Model 4 considers the earlier three variables as well as information about pastors. The results suggest that Black churches that have more formally educated, full-time pastors tend to sponsor more and varied programs. The final test (Model 5) includes all of the previous variables as well as indicators that describe church stance and worship elements. First, it reveals that churches where congregants are more frequently exposed to practical sermons tend to sponsor the wide-ranging types of programs considered here. However, churches where clergy frequently preach about spiritual strength are no more or less likely to offer cafeteria-style programs than their counterparts that preach on this subject less often. Yet Black churches that are social justice–oriented and those that attempt to assimilate new members quickly tend to sponsor more cafeteria-style programs as compared to those without these orientations.

The primary modeling take aways begin to inform us about the types of Black Church characteristics associated with the litany of programs and ministries *megachurches* are believed to sponsor. First, as church size increases so do the number and type of programs they provide to congregants and the community. Thus as concluded in anecdotal and qualitative work, size matters.[27] Furthermore, location matters. As might be expected, this pattern supports existing literature that shows that the needs found in urban spaces often influence how Black churches respond.[28] Moreover, Black churches that feature: formally educated, full-time pastors; practical sermons; a social justice focus; and, methods to assimilate new members efficiently also tend to offer cafeteria-style programs. Readers stumped by the "chicken-egg" dilemma (i.e., which comes first, church members or church programs) should be reminded of other studies that suggest the tendency of Black churches to respond to needs.[28] Although past research supports the current causal ordering, given the tendency of megachurches to organize niche groups and strive to *proactively* market to current members and visitors alike,[29] future research on this phenomenon may require new methodological assumptions and empirical approaches of inquiry. However, the broad generalizability of these findings[31] provides a foundation to further investigate Black megachurch programs and how they differ from those of both their large White counterparts and smaller Black congregations. Equally important, these results provide empirical support for earlier, largely anecdotal, descriptions about the relationship between megachurch resources and programs. They also help expand our knowledge about what will inevitably become the *Black megachurch tradition*.

Conclusion: The Black Megachurch as a Structural Force

Bolstered by charismatic leadership, a bold spiritual stance, aggressive marketing, diverse church cultural makeup, and substantial human and economic resources, I posit that Black megachurches position themselves as models of success. Salvation is believed to result in godly favor that should shape one's entire life. Each church investigated here directly or indirectly conveys this message. Pastors and/or co-pastors model success, other church leaders are expected to mirror this success— members are also expected to follow suit by emulating appropriate attitudes and behavior. The most extreme proponents embrace Prosperity theology and emphasize economic and physical blessings. However, most focus on spiritual benefits and the *possibility* of secular successes determined by an omniscient God. The stance of large Black churches is particularly salient when juxtaposed against a backdrop of Black history where blackness was not generally applauded and confident and successful Blacks were considered dangerous and uppity.

The vast majority of these congregations are intricately involved in a myriad of programs informed by educational imperatives at the international and national level. Despite critics that point to the negative repercussions of megachurch presence (i.e., traffic congestion, destroying suburban green space, undermining smaller congregations, sheep stealing),[32] for growing segments of the Black community, Black megachurches represent tangible proof of what Blacks can accomplish through tenacity, initiative, and godly validation. According to sample pastors, receiving salvation is one of the most important decisions in one's life. Yet with that choice comes certain expectations and equally important responsibilities that should ultimately result in Christians who will be impressive representatives of the all-powerful God they serve. Without ignoring social challenges in the Black community, the vast majority of sample congregations have been able to simultaneously develop church spaces that belie these harsh realities and offer a bevy of programs that confront them. By tapping into the strengths found in Black Church culture, the best elements of other Christian traditions, and dynamics from secular society, this group of Black megachurches is creating strategies of action[33] to ritualize desired attitudes and actions in order to cultivate victorious spiritual living and the potential for temporal blessings.

Table 1.1 Black Church Demographics and Religious and Practical Educational Programs by Size

	Average Sunday Attendance			
	Faith Factor Data			Current
	0–999	1,000–1,999	2,000+	Sample
% Yes or Designated Option				
Church and Clergy Demographics				
Baptist	93.7	4.3	2.0	50.0
Urban locale	63.5	83.3	78.6	56.3
Percent full-time pastor	75.5	97.1	100.0	100.0
Pastor has post-ministry degree	31.0	55.6	64.3	81.3
Sermons: practical advice (% always)	64.2	72.2	92.9	100.0
Sermons: spirituality (% always)	72.7	80.6	78.6	100.0
Sermons: Lib. theologies (% always)	13.0	11.4	7.1	31.3
Social justice environment (% always)	41.6	66.7	71.4	87.4
Church easily assimilates				
members (% very well)	37.2	47.2	71.4	87.4
Church Educational Programs (% Yes)				
Bible study other than Sunday school	97.7	94.4	100.0	100.0
Theological or doctrinal study	27.6	22.2	21.4	50.0
Prayer/mediation groups	92.5	100.0	92.9	100.0
Spiritual Retreats	63.4	80.6	78.6	50.0
Parenting/marriage enrichment	63.3	86.1	85.7	100.0
Youth programs	94.9	100.0	100.0	100.0
Young adult/singles programs	70.0	91.7	100.0	100.0
Tutoring/literacy programs	64.5	86.1	100.0	93.8
Voter registration or education	75.5	94.4	92.9	93.8
Employment training	43.7	66.7	71.4	93.8
Computer training	40.8	77.8	78.6	93.8
n	1786	36	14	16

Faith Factor 2000 data: N=1,863. Average Sunday Attendance: 0–3,500+. Note: Black megachurches from the Faith Factor 2000 data are identified in the third column as congregations with average Sunday attendance of at least 2,000 persons. Churches from this study are in the fourth column. Refer to the appendix for survey questions and response options.

Table 1.2: Summary of Linear Regression Models of Cafeteria-Style Programs Offered by National Sample of Black Churches

Modeling Question: Churches that reflect this feature (listed vertically in the left-most column) also tends to sponsor more of the 23 spiritual and secular programs than churches that do not have this feature? (Y="Yes")

	Model 1 *Denom.*	Model 2 *Church Size*	Model 3 *Location*	Model 4 *Pastor*	Model 5 *All Variables*
Baptist	Y	N	N	N	N
Church Size (Small to Megachurch Size)		Y	Y	Y	Y
Urban Location			Y	Y	Y
Pastor's Profile					
Pastor's Education (None to Doctorate)				Y	Y
Pastor is Fulltime				Y	Y
Church Dynamics					
Sermons often Focus on Practical Issues					Y
Sermons often Focus on Spirituality					N
Church has a Social Justice Environment					Y
Church Assimilates New Members Quickly					Y

Interpret each model vertically. All variables are statistically significant at $p < .05$ or greater. Faith Factor 2000 data. $N = 1,863$ Black churches. Denom.=denomination. Church size= 0 to 3,500+ attendees. Actual modeling output provided in the appendix.

Notes

1. Hartford Institute of Religious Research (2005), Thumma and Travis (2007), Tucker-Worgs (2002).
2. Formally educated pastors are the norm among Black megachurches, but less so among predominately White megachurches (Tucker 2002; Thumma and Travis 2007).
3. Gilbreath (1994), Lee (2007), Schaller (2000), Thumma and Travis (2007), Tucker (2002).
4. Dart (1991), Thumma and Travis (2007), Tucker (2002).
5. However, Niebuhr (1995a) suggests that the challenge megachurches ultimately face is succession once the charismatic pastor is no longer able to serve.
6. Refer to earlier work by Harrison (2005), Tucker-Worgs (2002), and Lee (2005).
7. Billingsley (1999), Drake and Cayton (1962), DuBois (1903[2003]), Frazier (1964), Lincoln (1984), Lincoln and Mamiya (1990).
8. Most readers know of Richard Allen and Absalom Jones as founders of the AME denomination in 1816. However, fewer persons may know about the other two figures. Lemuel Haynes (1753–1833) is considered the first Black man to be ordained in any denomination and he preached in White Congregationalist churches in New England. George Liele is credited with founding the first Black independent Baptist church in 1777 outside Savannah, Georgia (Allen 1960; Sernett 1985).
9. The following is a list of some of the research on the subject: Billingsley (1999), Drake and Cayton (1962), DuBois (1903[2003]), Ellison and Sherkat (1995), Frazier (1964), Lincoln (1984), Lincoln and Mamiya (1990), Morris (1984), and, Nelsen and Nelsen (1975).
10. Barnes (2004), Ellison and Sherkat (1995), Sherkat and Ellison (1991).
11. The Faith Factor data represent some of the more recent survey data on the Black Church. It includes 1,863 Black congregations of various sizes from the seven denominations typically used in research on Black religiosity as well as a small sample of Black megachurches (refer to the appendix for additional information on the national data file).
12. Thumma and Travis (2007).
13. Billingsley (1999), Cone (1995, 1969[1999]), Lincoln and Mamiya (1990).
14. Billingsley (1999), Lincoln and Mamiya (1990).
15. Results are based on 2007 census figures. Additionally, the non-Hispanic, single-race White population of 199.1 million represents 66 percent of the total population. The Hispanic population increased 1.4 million to reach 45.5 million as reported on July 1, 2007 (15.1 percent of the estimated total U.S. population of 301.6 million). Blacks are next at 40.7 million. The Native Hawaiian and Other Pacific Islander population is about 5.1 percent.
16. The 2006 figures show that about 9.8 percent (7.7 million) of the nation's families live in poverty. Increases in poor families mean continued feminization and juvenilization of poverty (Barnes 2005b; Fellmeth 2005; Johnson 2000; Peck and Segal

2006; Shipler 2004; U.S. Census 2007; Wilson 1996).

17. Only Hispanics, at 44 percent, experienced more illiteracy due largely to limited English proficiency. A review of racial/ethnic differences in high-school graduation rates shows that, in 2005, non-Hispanic Whites had the highest proportion of adults with a high school diploma or higher (91 percent), followed by Asians (87 percent), Blacks (81 percent), and Hispanics (59 percent).

18. In 2005, about 1.1 million Blacks age 25+ had advanced degrees such as Master's, Ph.D., M.D., or J.D degrees. According to 2006 figures, adults with advanced degrees earned four times more than those with less than a high-school diploma. In addition, adults that are 18 years old and older with Master's, professional, or doctoral degrees earned an average of $79,946, while those with less than a high school diploma earned about $19,915. Lastly, adults with a bachelor's degree earned an average of $54,689 in 2005; persons with a high school diploma earned $29,448.

19. Refer to *A First Look at the Literacy of America's Adults in the 21st Century* at http://nces.ed.gov/ssbr/pages/adultliteracy.asp?IndID=32: 2006 Census Report: Educational Attainment in the United States.

20. For example, according to a Johns Hopkins report published in 2007, race and class are mitigating factors associated with increased obesity in the United States such that 80 percent of Black women aged 40 years or over are overweight and 50 percent are obese. Black children have a higher prevalence for obesity than their White counterparts (Wang and Beydoun 2007). In addition, 2008 Centers for Disease Control figures show that 69.9, 67.1, 62.1, 59.6, and 38.7 percent of Black, American Indian, Hispanic, White, and Asians, respectively, are overweight or obese.

21. The uninsured rate for Asians declined from 17.2 percent in 2005 to 15.5 percent in 2006. The figures for Hispanics increased from 32.3 percent in 2005 to 34.1 percent in 2006. Blacks are also less likely than non-Blacks to visit comprehensive healthcare facilities, but are more likely to visit emergency rooms. They are also less likely to receive treatment at a private physician's office. These types of differences translate into life expectancies for Blacks that are five years less than those of Whites and Black infant mortality rates that have, since 1985, been twice as high as compared to White infants (Brown et al. 1999; Johnson 2000; Lykens and Jargowsky 2002; Potter and Klein-Rothschild 2002; Rodenborg 2004; U.S. Census 2007).

22. Blacks are twice as likely as Hispanics and eight times more likely than Whites to contract the disease. Blacks comprise about 50 percent of known AIDS cases (Centers for Disease Control 2002, 2003, 2004; MacMaster et al. 2007).

23. Barnes (2005c).

24. Additionally, 13 churches (81 percent) have CDCs and 10 (63 percent) currently receive faith-based funding or have been recipients previously.

25. Ibid., Schaller (2000), Vaugh (1993). These models only consider Sunday attendance rather than "weekend" as used in the megachurch definition suggested by

Thumma and Travis (2007).

26. In one of his list of 24 reasons for megachurch growth, Schaller (1990) suggests that their focus on attendance stands in stark contrast to emphasis on membership among long-established churches. He notes, "in scores of megachurches the average attendance is double or triple the membership total, while in some long-established smaller churches the membership total may be double the worship attendance" (p. 21).

27. Schaller (1990), Thumma and Travis (2007).

28. Barnes (2004, 2005), Billingsley (1999), Lincoln and Mamiya (1990), McRoberts (2003).

29. Refer to Barnes (2004, 2005, 2006). Casual order (i.e., is higher attendance a result of social programs or vice versa) was informed and justified by existing studies.

30. Refer to Schaller (2000) and Thumma and Travis (2007) about megachurch programs in general and Billingsley (1992, 1999), Tucker (2002), and Lincoln and Mamiya (1990) concerning Black churches or Black megachurches and the types of programs they provide.

31. Refer to Barnes (2004, 2005, 2006) for details regarding data constraints and other studies using this national data.

32. Thumma and Travis (2007).

33. Swidler (1986, 1995).

Chapter Two

Church Culture in Real Time

Worship as an Educational Tool

THE GLASS FRONT DOORS OF THE EDIFICE usher you into an expansive vestibule with travertine floors, a receptionist's area, and coffee shop in the corner. Greeters and a network of ushers all dressed in color-coordinated uniforms provide smiles, handshakes, welcomes, and worship bulletins. A throng of congregants mull around in this space, greeting each other, smiling, patiently yet expectantly awaiting the identically uniformed ushers to open the series of glass doors to the main sanctuary. Banter is barely audible as friends make small talk and update each other since their last encounter—their interaction is secondary to the primary objective of entering the sanctuary to get "a good seat." Some have already attended the earlier worship service and Sunday school and plan to remain for the second service; others await entry for the first time. As you move down the custom sisal carpeted aisle you notice vaulted ceilings, upper and lower arenas that easily seat several thousand each, and an expansive, platformed stage, decorated to emphasize the pulpit. An unobtrusive section houses hi-tech musical equipment to support the service without detracting from the pulpit. The backdrop behind the lectern is minimalist and includes a 10 foot cross-draped in cloth reflecting the liturgical calendar as well as an expansive world map flanked by white doves in flight. Brightly colored banners with messages such as "Jesus is Lord" or "Praise God" stream from the ceiling. Afrocentric art adorns the walls. The throng quietly seats itself in anticipation.

A praise team, rather than a traditional choir, ushers in the worship service. Six 50-inch screens positioned strategically around the sanctuary display song lyrics and announcements. A charismatic praise team leader, but not the senior pastor, spearheads a series of spirited congregational, gospel-based songs then renders a fervent prayer. Using call-and-response, the praise leader encourages the congregation to become fully involved in the praise and worship portion of the service: as evidence of their adoration of God; in response to previous blessings; in expectation of future favor; and, in preparation for the sermon. A sign language interpreter relays this message and other information throughout the service. Praise dancers wearing brightly adorned, flowing gowns raise banners and outstretched hands to the heavens. All of these events result in jubilant singing, dancing, clapping, and often, shouting. A period to welcome visitors often referred to as "Passing the Peace" and corporate prayer follow. Two additional gospel songs are sung by the 200 person adult choir who are also dressed in robes that coordinate with the sanctuary colors.

All these activities are preparation for the focus of the worship service—presentation of the Word of God by the senior pastor. As he or she rises or enters, a cacophony of applause ensues. The senior pastor instructs the congregation to "give God a hand clap of praise." The senior pastor may lead the congregation in a song, provide words of welcome and thanksgiving or simply offer a short prayer before beginning the sermon. As the message unfolds, the congregation is both enthralled and captivated by the charismatic eloquence of the pastor's words and gestures. A scriptural passage is exegeted. The sermon may reflect a detailed presentation of a few verses, be a continuation of an ongoing series, or strategically link an array of passages to a broad theme. In addition to analyzing and explaining the chosen text(s), the pastor challenges, exhorts, and sometimes chastises listeners regarding their responsibilities as women and men of God as well as the corresponding rewards they should expect now and in the future. Symbolism is often used to draw parallels between the experiences of Blacks in the Diaspora with those of the Israelites—God's biblically chosen people.

The sermon detail is balanced by its inspirational nature as the pastor deftly commands language to convey a message of triumph and hope. It is also a captivating experience in story-telling. However, it is not uncommon for the sermon to be periodically interrupted by hand clapping, "amens," shouts, and short musical interludes. The sermon climaxes as the pastor reminds the congregation of Christ's ultimate sacrifice for them and the favor, confidence, power, peace, boldness, faith, godly lifestyle, and commitment to the church's mission that such knowledge should engender. Following the Lord's Supper, service ends with the invitation to discipleship, more communal singing, and a closing prayer to safeguard persons until they meet again. The pastor jokingly challenges people not to "lose their religion" in the parking lot and to be considerate of other drivers as they exit. Congregants again exchange pleasantries, hug visitors and friends, smile, share agreement regarding the powerful nature of the sermon, and exit the sanctuary. Some move quickly to niche meetings; others progress toward the parking lot. Church leaders prepare for the next worship service scheduled to begin shortly.

Similar worship experiences may occur in Christian churches across the country on any given Saturday or Sunday morning. What makes the above composite illustration unique is its scale, grandeur, precision, and uniquely Black Church flavor.[1] This type of worship service reflects a fusion of elements from the historic Black Church tradition, evangelical White Church as well as particularistic dimensions based on each church's unique history, identity, denomination, and theological stance. The above model is dynamic—some Black megachurches have built new edifices in suburban locales while others have expanded on an historic urban site. Some continue to include traditional choirs, deacons, and other holdovers from the historic Black Church. Praise teams and lay leaders are more common in others. The Lord's Supper and baptism are always commemorated.[2]

Despite heterogeneity, Sunday/weekend services appear to flow aimlessly and belie the complex set of organized, highly efficient, interdependent networks of clergy and members under the leadership of a charismatic senior pastor. Moreover, Sunday service is often the pinnacle event for smaller congregations. And although central to its life blood, for Black megachurches, Sunday worship *services* are part of a myriad of worship, outreach, engagement, fellowship, business, and teaching programs, as well as alliances and networks that took place the prior week and that will occur during the next. In addition to being inspirational, my findings uncover the instructional dimensions of worship services. I contend that no gathering is fortuitous; each is an opportunity to cultivate a specific set of church beliefs and expectations. Although Black Church culture has been defined and described in earlier chapters, it is equally important to examine how cultural tools are *experienced*. I rely on pastoral sermons and participant observation to illustrate the educational aspects of the worship experience, usage of Black Church cultural tools and church-specific cultural components. Results show that worship is about praise, but it is also about expectations, preparation for volunteerism, and a certain kind of lifestyle outside church walls.

Scripture, Sermons, and Black Church Culture

An impressive body of anecdotal and ethnographic work in religious studies, sociology, cultural studies, and Black/African American studies confirm how "the Book" continues to shape the lives of Black Christians.[3] Scriptural readings during devotionals, responsive readings, and sermonic references provide written authority of God's presence, power, and purpose in the lives of believers. For some people, scriptural interpretations reflected in the weekly sermon reflect, to a large degree, a message directly to them from God—through their pastor. Thus one of the dynamics that make Black Church clergy so potentially influential is linked to their ability to preach. Cone (1997) eloquently describes this process:

> In black preaching, the Word becomes embodied in the rhythm and the emotions of language as the people respond bodily to the Spirit in their midst. The

black sermon arises out of the totality of the people's existence—their pain and joy, trouble and ecstasy. When the Word is spoken as truth and the people feel the presence of truth in the midst of their troublesome situation, they respond to the preached word by ratifying it with resounding "Amens." (P. 18)

So by default, pastors who know how to "preach the Word" have a unique position in Black churches—regardless of church size. It has long been said that, in Black churches, the pastor is God's proxy on earth. And his or her ability to convey an exciting, informative, and engaging sermon is proof of his or her godly calling. Although quality preaching may be considered one sign of a cleric's calling, it can also result in increased status if effective preaching is associated with formal education or the ability to deftly manipulate scripture. However, my findings suggest that biblical interpretation in the form of the sermon takes on a unique meaning among Black megachurches. Just as these churches model success, congregational expectations for weekly exemplary sermons (as well as pastor-led bible studies) are high. Black megachurch pastors are expected to raise the roof. Each aspect of the liturgical worship service sets the stage for the climax—the sermon. And members often take great pride in bragging rights about their pastor's singular speaking skills, so much so that remarks such as, "pastor Smith said this or that" are just as frequently heard as "the bible states this or that."

It has been suggested that megachurch sermons tend to focus on practical issues and real-world examples that can be applied to one's daily life. This sermonic style is also common among the sample Black megachurches. Oratory of the past has been replaced by listener-friendly pastoral tales, current events, references to movies and music, and other nontraditional rhetorical devices that resonate with media-swamped listeners in tune with popular culture.[4] However, careful review—including content, format, and style—uncovers elements of Black Church culture as well as rhetorical devices that provide and reinforce instructional guidelines for empowered spiritual and practical living. Regardless of denomination, the sermon represents the primary teaching/learning tool during worship. The following representative quote, provided by a pastor of a Midwestern church affiliated with the

United Church of Christ emphasizes the importance of preaching, rather than its speaker: "Carter G. Woodson said in 1903, there are three elements that are chief in Black churches—preaching, music, and the Holy Spirit. He did not say, *a certain preacher* [emphasis is his], he said preaching." A pastor from the Baptist faith in Washington, D.C., echoes the above remark as well as his understanding of the relationship between Black Church theology, preaching, and outcomes:

> The theology of the church in relationship to a particular local church is framed and formed through the preaching of the Gospel every Sunday. Now whether we say it or not, we are really molding minds and affecting the hearts and the spirits of a congregation.

According to this pastor, the objectives of worship service are multifaceted and include consistently presenting and reinforcing church theology to ultimately shape the attitudes and actions of congregants. Sermons include an inspirational component as well as biblical instruction. By exposing a captive audience each week to the pastor's understanding of her or his calling and scriptural interpretations, attendees are being socialized about the church's theology, identity, and position in the community. In addition to acknowledging the multi-leveled instructional dimensions of preaching, a common response focuses on the *type* of preaching that should occur:

> From [pastor's name] teachings and from the scriptures…the church is…seeking to move beyond the traditional Baptist church—just coming to hear the sermon, hear the choir, and go home…we wanted to make the scriptures so relevant to our lives…it's like, let's take this Word of God, let's look at it and let's apply it to our lives. (clergy representative from a Baptist church in Atlanta)

For these clergy, scripture should be interpreted such that it is germane to listeners. Paralleling observations by Harrison (2005), the above cleric believes that his church has surpassed many of its denominational peers based on the nature of the worship experience and the quality of biblical instruction. As suggested by a pastor of a Baptist church in Kentucky, no subject is outside the domain of a pastor who is in tune with the concerns and needs of the congregation:

I've got sermons that I preached on health and nutrition…I preached a sermon on Women's Day about Jesus and fitness. It was a series entitled, 'Jesus Grew, How about You?'…I preached a sermon about how Blacks are not taking care of themselves physically and how Black women have problems with obesity that contributes to high blood pressure.

Sermons are expected to cover the gamut of experiences expected by Christians who are in the world, but not of it. Discerning pastors who are able to anticipate and respond to issues as practical as health, as economically salient as wealth acquisition and home ownership, and as potentially sensitive as relationships and sexuality, are best poised to meet congregational needs, respond to community concerns, foresee niche group demands, convincingly articulate a godly vision, and ultimately cause church growth.

In his biographical account of Bishop T.D. Jakes, Lee (2005) describes the "American" preacher's mastery and use of religious, scholarly, pop culture, and experiential material during commanding sermons. Similarly, among this sample, rhetorical devices such as rhyming, lyricism, and appropriation of secular jargon are strategically included in sermons to help listeners remember the primary sermonic points, challenge listeners to apply them, and convince listeners that they can. Analysis of pastoral sermons uncovered traditional biblical exegesis interspersed with practical application germane to the Black experience.[5] Sermons are not preached in a stoic, scholarly fashion, but rather in a format to confirm the pastor's attentiveness to specific challenges facing listeners and knowledge of world and community events. Common sermonic subjects that parallel sociological inquiry on the Black experience include single Black females' inability to find appropriate husbands (i.e., the marriageable male dilemma); Black male incarceration; sexuality and Black male–female relationships;[6] economic challenges linked to the inability to pay one's rent; home loss; and racism and discrimination.[7]

Black Church cultural tools such as Black gospel music, biblical interpretation that centers the Black experience, and call-and-response are also integral to worship experiences. Their use illustrates the continued influence of an historical tool kit. However, Black megachurches also avail themselves of cultural components from other religious traditions and secular society, re-appropriate these tools, and make them their own. According to Niebuhr (1995), megachurch worship centers on "electric bands playing contemporary music, its dramatic skits and its sermons that focus on the tough issues of everyday living" (p. 1) that critics associate with entertainment. A somewhat more culturally relative assessment suggests that such congregations attempt to inform and instruct in ways that are interesting and exciting to congregants which "means strategizing to discover the right contemporary wrapper (music, for one) in which to present a timeless Gospel message"(Niebuhr 1995: 2).

Common Cultural Concepts and Contemporary Christology

In addition to revamping existing ones, the sample congregations created new tools specific to their church demographics, leadership styles, and neighborhood contexts. This section describes several cultural components that continually emerged in this analysis that I contend shape Black megachurch socialization processes: *Kingdom Building, favor,* and contemporary images of Christ. The first concept suggests that biblical examples of "heaven" should be emulated on earth in the collective and individual lives of believers. Furthermore, establishing God's kingdom on earth should result in a more godly society. Victorious living for Christians should be distinct and "better" than that of non-Christians; scripture provides clear instruction to meet these objectives. According to the pastor of a nondenominational church in Indiana, the Lord's Prayer is applicable beyond its literal interpretation:

> When the disciples asked Jesus, 'How should we pray?' He said…'Our father in heaven, hallowed be your name, your kingdom come and your will be done on earth.' And so we focus a lot on bringing heaven to earth—that's a core theology of our church—that you should experience heaven on earth.

For him, experiencing God's kingdom on earth should manifest in economic empowerment, spiritual maturity, the absence of illness, and victory over life's challenges. Kingdom Building also usually includes a strong community component such that believers aspire for personal empowerment without neglecting social problems. Biblically-based, expected outcomes are usually tangible (i.e., education, home owner-ship, or being debt- and disease-free). Most pastors teach members to expect positive results as they center God in their efforts to successful-ly negotiate secular society and literally alter the spaces in which they travel. In this way, otherworldly tenets inform this-worldly expecta-tions. Kingdom Building is at the heart of the theological perspective of several churches. For most, it is one of a set of cultural tools interwoven in a broader church vision and framing process.

Just as practical references indicative of megachurch culture are evi-dent, so are rhetorical devices associated with the historic Black Church. Cone (1997) describes both the transcendent nature of the preached moment and its practical dimensions:

> The "Amen" is the congregation's witness to, and participation in, the procla-mation. It is their Yes that lets the preacher know that he or she is on the "right track," affirming that they know the truth about what is preached. At this point the Word of truth transcends conceptual analysis and becomes a liberat-ing event wherein the people are moved to another level of existence, and they are permitted to experience a foretaste of the New Jerusalem. (P. 18)

Applying Cone's (1997) interpretation to these Black megachurch expe-riences suggests yet another implication of the Kingdom Building process where the sermon provides biblical instruction as well as a metaphorical glimpse of the very *heaven* pastors believe they are charged to bring to earth. This "foretaste" becomes the template that informs very real efforts to achieve excellence as a church member, in one's personal life, and in church program offerings. Generally during the sermon con-clusion, ecstatic displays (sometimes referred to as the "hoop") can occur that include symbolic references to the omnipotence, omniscience, and omnipresence of God. However, references to God as a "doctor in a sickroom," "lawyer in a courtroom," "lawyer who has never lost a case," or a "God who sits high and looks low"—historically common during many a Black pastor's sermonic climax—have been supplanted by Black megachurch pastoral challenges to remember and live as right-ful recipients of God's goodwill, take back assets stolen by the devil, and break spiritual and emotional chains. These contemporary statements still result in call-and-response as listeners stand in agreement with the preacher's statements.

One of the hardest truths to convey to a historically oppressed, disenfranchised, and devalued group is their inherent worth. Couple feelings of inadequacy and invisibility with religious doctrine that often associates "righteousness" with "works" and you have a recipe for disempowerment. However, quite possibly one of the most noteworthy socializing processes evident among Black megachurches is the ability to convince congregants, not only of their *worth*, but of their *worthiness* for abundance and success in their many forms. This dynamic is summarized by the concept *favor*. Although mentioned in earlier parts of this book, the frequency of its use merits further attention. Broadly defined, favor refers to God-given benefits the saved possess that their unsaved counterparts do not. This spiritual sanctioning enables them to lead godly lives and expect certain outcomes. Although it is available to all Christians, clergy contend that most believers do not fully experience God's favor because they fail to avail themselves of it. Furthermore, refusing to follow godly dictates can also undermine one's ability to fully experience these benefits. Favor is often associated with congregations that espouse Prosperity theology and more broadly with churches that embrace neo-Pentecostalism. Although the vast majority of the sample Black megachurches are not Prosperity proponents, some understanding of divine entitlement is evident in sermons and other teaching/learning events.

Harrison's (2005) case study of a Word of Faith church details the narrowest understanding of favor:

> Harvest is the financial and material prosperity God wishes to transfer from the hands of the sinner and bestow upon the righteous, that is, those bold, overcoming Christians who are unafraid to name and claim what is rightfully theirs as members of the body of Christ. (P. 4)

For Prosperity adherents, fully experiencing God's favor requires a type of mapping process from the surreal to the real—informed by a specific doctrine and acculturation process. Harrison (2005) continues:

The teaching...encourages self-actualization and upward socioeconomic mobility while supplying a belief system that supports that process. This belief system and the accompanying worldview provide followers with a message of personal empowerment that helps them negotiate the potential tensions or sense of dislocation and alienation that may arise...(P. 54)

In *Money Thou Art Loosed!*, Prosperity preacher Thompson (1999) presents a much more provocative prescription for tapping into the material dimensions of favor:

He [referring to God] then told me that we have authority over money and can make demands on money and that money would obey us....Your having money is important to God. Your having money with the right intentions and attitudes will put you in position to walk in the fullness of His abundance for you and be a blessing to others. But, most importantly, your prosperity will glorify God....Our destiny is divine prosperity....It is predestined, foreordained, and predetermined that God's children should have more than enough. And as soon as we learn how to cooperate with His Word and get into His flow, money will not be a problem for us; we will be walking in divine prosperity. (Pp. i–ii, 8–9)

This same author provides a formula for experiencing this covenant arrangement that requires believers to be resocialized based on a laundry list of principles that, once followed, will make money obey them. Although most clergy interviewed here find this stance absurd, they hold to certain tenets that, I contend, have been incorrectly associated with Prosperity theology, but still reflect the notion of godly favor. References to Deuteronomic passages when the Israelites are promised their enemies' land as part of God's covenant; New Testament assurances of receipt of "all these things" as one first seeks God's kingdom; and, the implications of becoming prosperous as one's soul does each suggest a correlation between Christian living and blessings.

Most clergy here espouse a more subtle and nuanced understanding of favor. They still conclude that Christians often function beneath their godly privileges and that God *can and wants* to reward those who prioritize Christian living and ministry appropriately. Representative sermonic quotes illumine how this concept is often framed. For example, in the sermon, "God Wants You Rich!," the pastor of a non-denominational church in the Midwest supports the spiritual impetus of favor, focuses on its more tangible manifestations, and locates such entitlement in the most common contexts; "when you say 'God bless you,' you are really proclaiming, producing, and actually invoking the favor of God on that person's life." In "What Favor Looks Like," a pastor of a Baptist church in Virginia references Nehemiah 2:1–10 in a series of messages focused on living beyond all limits:

> Out of the experiences one can have…none of them equal having the favor of God to rest in your life…the person who lives in the favor of God is like a stick dipped in honey…the favor of God just sticks to them…[defines favor—when] …others are inclined to help you and cooperate with you even if they don't like you…God steadfastly and sovereignly choosing to place His hand of blessing on your life.

However, like most clergy in this study, this pastor is intentional about couching his description of favor such that it does not preclude potential problems believers may face—yet he still emphatically and eloquently concludes that godly favor is the most important blessing a Christian can experience:

> If favor means that behind every negative is a positive, I want favor. If favor means behind every wound there will be a wonder, I want favor. If favor means underneath a burden there will be a hidden blessing, I want favor. If favor means behind every dark cloud I can depend on a silver lining, I want favor. If favor means alongside every frustration there will be inspiration and motivation, then I want favor to rest on my life.

Furthermore, divine preference does not necessarily require personal material success because the resources that *others possess* are at one's disposal. This same pastor continues:

> You can achieve more and accomplish more with favor…you can have a pocket full of money and still have doors slammed in your face. Favor is better than money because you can be dead broke and doors will be opening up for you everywhere. Favor can do things that money and things can't do. Money can buy you a house, but favor can get you approved with jacked-up credit. Money can pay your bills, but favor can make sure your needs are met until you find the next job. Money can buy medical insurance, but favor can get you healed when you can't afford the co-pay or the prescription.

Unlike Prosperity proponents, this explanation suggests that the needs of believers will be met despite their socioeconomic status. Moreover, by referencing challenging scenarios that resonate with many Blacks such as unemployment, credit problems, and healthcare challenges, the supernatural is tied to everyday experiences as theology is broadly informed by sociology. Belief in godly favor can act as a compelling catalyst for optimism and proactive behavior that is particularly important for congregants experiencing great hardship, but who are cognizant of the wealth and stability other church members are experiencing. Because based on favor, when God blesses their *neighbors*, it means that God is in the *neighborhood*—and thus their blessings are on the way.

The pastor of an AME church on the West Coast presents a cautionary tale of Christian entitlement gone awry as a challenge to establish proper priorities. The sermon "Let Us Review the Mystery of Chronic Dissatisfaction" reflects a mastery of scripture, stories, language, and cadence associated with the historic Black Church combined with practicality, current events, and musicology associated with contemporary megachurches:

> Let us consider the mystery of chronic dissatisfaction. Touch somebody and say, "I can't get no satisfaction"…[It] seems as though for some of us, no matter how the Lord blesses us, we're never satisfied—gotten the promotion, gotten the love of your life, many of your dreams have come true, many things that God has blessed us with have come to pass, yet there is a feeling of dissatisfaction….When is enough, enough—No matter how the Lord blesses…you have the house, the car, the position and we still feel unhappy…we ask, 'what in the world is keeping me in this chronic state of dissatisfaction?'…yet some people feel satisfaction in spite of their failings, in spite of their conflicts, and in spite of their problems….Dissatisfaction is Satan putting into our spirit the desire for the next level, the new model, for something else…convincing us if we just had the newest this or a little bit more, our lives would be complete…but if you don't have God in your life, you will always suffer from chronic dissatisfaction.

Although he does not necessarily find the acquisition of possessions problematic, by weaving in scenarios such as the suicides of successful Black performers Phyllis Hyman and Donny Hathaway, the hymn, "Count Your Blessings," Mick Jagger's popular "I Can't Get No

Satisfaction," and call and response—this pastor evokes images of Citizen Kane's heartrending call for his beloved Rosebud to admonish listeners about the dangers of unchecked materialism. Most important- ly he suggests a tipping point after which unbridled expectations become sacrilegious.

In general, clergy consensus suggests that favor is: bestowed by God; an entitlement of believers that is not always experienced; possi- bly but not necessarily material in nature; and, not bartered based on works, but requires godly living and learning to be fully understood. Prosperity proponents tend to espouse a causal relationship between positive confession, unwavering faith, and success in matters of health and wealth. They are in the numeric minority in this study. Yet belief in godly favor is common where most clergy *correlate* Christian living, bible study, prayer, volunteerism, godly responses to negative experi- ences, and the character these situations build to the potential for a myriad of blessings. And the manner in which favor is presented pro- vides an empowering context to transform the attitudes and behavior of a people who have experienced both a history of ill treatment *and* vic- tories despite seemingly insurmountable odds.

The final cultural tool focuses on depictions of the salvation story. In terms of process, sermonic concepts, themes, and stories inevitably progress toward references to "the cross" and Christ's death, burial, and resurrection as evidence of humanity's value and potential power to experience victorious living. This pattern is most evident among Baptist churches. During these presentations, Jesus is positioned as the quintessential leader. His multifaceted nature means depictions of a suffering Savior followed by those of a victorious Messiah are just as palatable to listeners. Images of "Christ the muscular carpenter who could talk the plain talk of Jewish peasants and toss around the money changers' table" described in Niebuhr's (1995: 2) op-ed piece on megachurches renders Jesus larger than life and foretells His messianic promise. However, the latter writer's implications that this version of Christ is endemic to *contemporary large churches* does not take into account the understanding of Christ in historic Black religious circles described by scholars such as Cone (1997), West (1982), Wilmore (1994), and other Black researchers who have presented a more radical, prophetic version of Christ. According to their assessments, it is not a stretch to conclude that Black megachurch nuanced representations of Jesus reflect, to a large degree, appropriations of historic Black Church images.

In addition to reinforcing an image of Christ that is discerning, dramatic, and sensitive (among other features), each reference to the salvific act reinforces both the importance of congregations of predominately Black Christians and their inheritance—despite the world's less favorable assessments. Sermons reflect both music and message. During each worship service they further confirm the pastor's appropriateness as leader and the need to be personally committed to church ministry. Sermons also reinforce the ability to think and live "big" spiritually and in many cases, literally, as evidenced by the existence and efforts of the very churches in which they are preached. Moreover, it is equally important that these same expectations and explanations are modeled by the pastor as she or he engages, shapes, and even alters Black Church culture.

Corporate Worship: Neo-Pentecostalism and Beyond

Lincoln and Mamiya's (1990) prediction of an increase in neo-Pentecostalism among Black churches, made less than two decades ago, has occurred—particularly among Black megachurches. Although it reflects a variety of features, common characteristics of neo-Pentecostalism include emphasis on charismatic worship services and preaching, the urging of the Holy Spirit, and expectations of spiritual and secular success. Some writers posit a fourth characteristic that requires a balance between spirituality and social action. Historically associated with "lower-class" churches, neo-Pentecostalism is increasingly embraced by middle-class Black congregations, especially Methodist and Baptist denominations.[8]

Because neo-Pentecostalism is associated with high-energy, cathartic worship, and in some instances, healing and miracles, it promises a church experience distinct from traditionalism and routinization typically associated with denominationalism. Given the challenges some Blacks face in the larger society, scholars argue that neo-Pentecostalism helps to cultivate spaces where participants welcome spiritual release and anticipate personal success. Although some critics accuse the neo-Pentecostal movement of undermining a Black Church activist focus on social problems such as poverty, proponents provide the following counter: "the best antidote to poverty is not to be a poor person" (Rivera 2002: 2). The primary distinction between the viewpoints of the two camps appears to be how social action should occur. Historic Black Church activists tended to focus on challenging negative systemic problems (i.e., structural forces); neo-Pentecostal supporters tend to focus on individual initiative (i.e., agency). This upsurge in interest is also important here because, for Black megachurches that now embrace neo-Pentecostalism, it represents an unexpected way of understanding what is appropriate worship and how Christianity should play out in the lives of believers. Particularly among more traditionally staid and pragmatic denominations, appropriating neo-Pentecostalism means re-socializing and re-educating congregants to praise, think, behave, and live differently. Black churches that have most successfully introduced this perspective seem to be experiencing significant growth or revitalization. During a sermon from a pastor of a Baptist church in the Midwest, dimensions of this worship experience are used as a metaphor for a broader Christian edict to live godly:

> There's an African proverb that says that when you strike one side of a drum the entire drum vibrates [asks percussionist to demonstrate]…when you strike the left side of the drum, the right side of the drum will feel the impact. When Christ strikes you on Sunday morning—like this choir and we feel the anointing and the power of His presence, then guess what, Monday should vibrate also…you get struck on Sunday, then your relationship [with God] should vibrate. Every area of your life should vibrate when Christ strikes you.

Historic Black Church worship has been described as corporate, cathartic, and because of dynamics associated with racism, counterbalancing. Its spiritual dimensions are clear. However, the more practical implications may not be as evident for persons unfamiliar with its multidimensionality. For example, Battle (2006) writes: "the Black Church reminds the world about many of God's children, whom many are inclined to forget. And...restore[s] through worship and prayer the image of God among all persons" (p. 44). According to Cone (1972), the same Blacks who frequented juke joints on Saturday night could be found praising God in the sanctuary Sunday morning. Existing studies also describe the intentionality by which megachurches strategically incorporate a myriad of spiritual and secular dynamics:

> The worship forms and styles used within these churches are shaped by the larger secular culture....Megachurches take worldly movies, music, television programs, commercials, and pop trends and baptize them into the service of the kingdom...as such, the message of these megachurches appeals to a larger and more diverse audience than traditional churches. (Thumma and Travis 2007: 140–41)

These same authors describe, "considerable variation within the worship service" (p. 27). Although this type of worship variability might be associated with megachurches in general, it is not new to the Black Church. Scholars, theologians, and musicologists such as Cone (1969[1999], 1972), Dubois (1903 [2003]), Lincoln and Mamiya (1990), and Costen (1993) provide convincing, vivid portraits of historic worship styles and content to show how they were influenced by factors such as denomination, congregational class makeup, the pastor's profile, and the varied experiences of Blacks in the larger society. An equally important and potentially overriding element of worship service for many Blacks was and continues to be the influence of the Holy Spirit. I posit that expanded worship options and experiences found among Black megachurches reflect, to a large degree, contemporary variations on an old tradition where Black churches were expected to meet a variety of desires and concerns (whether they have been successful has been debated). These diverse expectations were no exception for the large churches I investigated.

As found in earlier studies, multiple weekend worship services are the norm among the sample congregations. Several services enable churches to create niche worship events for their diverse populace, for others, separate services are necessary for logistical purposes. In a substantial number of churches, one pattern shows somewhat older members attending earlier services and younger persons and young couples attending later services. I attribute this tendency to both practical and generational reasons. First, earlier worship services tend to be, by default, shorter in length and more sermon-focused in order to allow sufficient time for Sunday school, bible study, or subsequent worship services. Later services (particularly the last service of the day), are generally less bound by time constraints on how long worship can be held. Moreover, despite a generally high-energy worship experience, earlier services seemed to be somewhat more subdued as compared to the highly charismatic, voluble tenor of latter services. Although Saturday services are uncommon among the sample Black megachurches, two to four Sunday services and a mid-week service are normative. Irrespective of denomination, worship is energetic and typically indicative of neo-Pentecostalism. Unlike many historic Black churches, worship service is typically initiated by a praise team rather than church leaders such as deacons. Despite the use of praise teams, every church, save one, also has multiple choirs. It is common to see 100–200 member choirs in addition to 10–15 singers positioned upfront at designated microphones. Furthermore, the types and placement of songs illustrate syncretism. Praise team worship is generally a fusion of syncopated White anthems[9] and Black gospel music. However, choral renditions tend to be historic and contemporary gospel music by Black artists.[10] Spirituals are sung less frequently.

Other holdovers from the historic Black tradition include the inclusion of a congregational song and, as mentioned earlier, call-and-response sprinkled throughout services. However, this latter activity moves beyond the traditional "amen" and takes on a particularly important role to both foster interactions between the pulpit and congregants as well as *across* the congregation. By frequently asking congregants to "tell your neighbor *this or that*," pastors reinforce key sermonic elements or interject levity into the sermon, personally engage the masses, and provide intermittent moments for people to "get to know" pew members. Although this device is used in other Black churches, the observed frequency among Black megachurches suggests that it also reflects a strategy used by pastors to create welcoming congregational spaces in settings that, based on size, can be impersonal.[11] The offering is also considered part of the *worship* experience, accompanied by clapping and instructions to bring one's gifts into the storehouse. Just as people are taught to expect blessings, they are socialized to freely give to the church. In several cases, offerings are given during hierarchical processionals with tithers first in line and nontithers escorted later. Despite congregational size, communal prayer and the Lord's Supper are always included. Also frequent and linked to the megachurch phenomena is the use of praise dancers of both sexes and various ages.[12]

Several other specific services further illustrate ways in which Black megachurches incorporate aspects of secular society during worship, praise, and proselytizing efforts. First, the role of popular culture as a strategy to attract children and youth is apparent. For increasing numbers of Black youth, "keeping it real"[13] means expressing themselves in ways that are personally authentic—and distinct from White and/or Black middle-class culture. As explained by Hall (1983), for youth, "Black popular culture is a contradictory space..." (p. 26) where "'good Black popular culture can pass the test of authenticity—the reference to Black experience and to Black expressivity" (p. 28). One would expect youth who embrace this view to be conflicted as they try to understand how they "fit" and whether to challenge aspects of the status quo, such as organized religion, in search of activities that resonate with their experiences.

Most of the sample Black megachurches understand this dilemma and are intentionally, proactively attempting to address it. For example, during 10:45 A.M. Youth Sunday at a Baptist church in Kentucky,[14] the sanctuary is decorated with life-sized, two-dimensional images of superheroes to reinforce the theme that youth can be superheroes for Christ. A choir of about 200 youth is dressed to complement the occasion. Some wear superhero customs. Yet most of the older teens are adorned in blue jeans and "bling bling." Youth clergy lead the service and the youth choir renders songs interspersed with gospel rap lyrics. The intentional inclusion of gospel rap music and dancing[15] illustrate the extent the church will take to create a space that "meets young people where they are"—all fostered by the pastor's call to counter negative street culture using a Gospel message. Moreover, technology is innovatively used as the church lights are dimmed for a candle-lit period of singing. However, rather than lighting candles, church and choir members illuminate the sanctuary by turning on and raising their cellular telephones.

Similarly, in a United Church of Christ congregation located in Chicago, the rapper Common is featured in an impromptu rap session as youth engage in a collective group dance, the Electric Slide, during the closing of a December 31st Watch Night service. Moreover, a Sunday youth service at a Baptist congregation in Philadelphia features youth worship leaders, a teen Praise Team, children's choir, a drum team, youth dancers, and a step troupe akin to those that perform during step shows at HBCUs.[16] However, as described by the following pastor, these type of youth outreach efforts must include a practical teaching component:

> How does Jesus becoming flesh and dwelling among us connect with a 15-year-old...a teacher asks a kid, 'Should we teach safe sex or should we teach abstinence?' The 15-year-old said, 'Well, if you want to save our souls, then teach us abstinence.' And all the kids said, 'Amen. Amen.' Then he said, 'But if you want to save our lives, you better teach us how to put on a condom.' Now what does the Gospel say about that? Because otherwise I become so heavenly focused it does no earthly good. (pastor from urban Midwestern congregation)

Targeted programs for the young as well as wholesome activities they consider "cool" can reinforce the bible, facilitate teamwork as well as discipline and help build comradery. Moreover, the message of "whosoever will" is evident during open calls for youth participation where body type, social status, or aptitude does not preclude youth involvement. During these events, one's level of commitment drives progress. Beyond their religious import, such activities can provide critical sociopsychological benefits as youth engage in activities like those found in school settings, but for a variety of reasons, they may be unable to participate.[17] In addition to attracting and maintaining youth involvement, these activities foster church commitment by parents. The intentionality shown to youth by Black megachurches here is indicative of Negro Church efforts described by Dubois (1903 [2003]), later by Mays and Nicholson (1933), and by Lincoln and Mamiya (1990). And just as BET programs such as the Bobby Jones Gospel Show now reflect a more contemporary edge, *newer* comers such as Co Co Brother, host of Lift Every Voice, Rev. Run of Run's House, as well as pastor Jamal Bryant's youth empowerment summits and tours out of Baltimore, Maryland, are catering to a more youthful Christian audience and expanding their understanding of worship and *authentic* Christian living. In this way "keeping it real" means candidly, proactively, and purposefully establishing "church *creeds*" that are just as aggressive as those found in the street.

These congregations avail themselves of terminology, iconography, activities, and technology from popular culture, the historic Black Church, and White evangelical spaces. What is considered profane is debatable—particularly where Black youth are concerned. The *spiritual* and *secular* intentionally and strategically meet in a space designed to capture the attention and imagination of attendees of all ages and backgrounds. These types of nontraditional approaches that challenge prevailing norms about what constitutes "worship" are part and parcel of what scholars suggest uniquely characterize some of today's megachurches.[18] The sample congregations are not afraid to take elements that may be considered secular (i.e., music, dance, language forms) and make them spiritual in order to proselytize, speak to concerns, and provide solutions. They also feel empowered by the belief that there is little that cannot be appropriated to further the Gospel message and help people live successful lives. Interestingly, the vast majority of the churches studied here do not espouse Prosperity theology, but rather tactically infuse teaching and learning activities with the message that God *can provide* abundance to believers who live godly lives and invoke their personal agency to experience success. This type of approach may not be unique to the Black megachurch. However, the boldness that comes with size and success appear to make their environments more fertile for such experiences, expressions, and educational strategies.

Like their White counterparts, corporate worship in the Black megachurch includes technology and cultural markers from secular society. However, for the latter congregations profiled here, these cultural tools are not overshadowed by historic Black Church cultural components such as Black gospel music, call-and-response, ecstatic praise, social justice themes, and scriptural redaction germane to the Black experience. To illustrate this point, I reference several data sources to compare and contrast worship experiences for Black churches of various sizes as well as predominately White megachurches.[19] Although all the same worship indicators are not present across the two data sources, readers are able to assess several differences between Black and predominately White Church worship styles—particularly for megachurches. I am interested in substantive rather than statistical differences in worship expressions such as sermon content, music, and worship-related instruction.

As presented in Table 2.1 (Panel 1), a strong pattern is apparent for the five types of sermons. As church size increases for Black churches, so does the percentage of churches that "always" incorporate these sermons. For example, about 83 percent of Black churches with average Sunday worship attendance of 999 or fewer people are always exposed to sermons about God's love and care. The exposure rate is about 92 percent for churches with an average attendance of 1,000–1,999 persons. However, 100 percent of the Black megachurches in the national sample and the churches studied here always emphasize God's love and care during sermons. Yet according to Thumma and Travis' (2007) results, only about 44 percent of primarily White megachurches frequently focus on this theme. Frequent exposure to sermons that include practical advice among Black churches in the national sample are as follows: 64 percent for smaller churches, 72 percent for moderately sized churches, and almost 93 percent for Black megachurches. The rate is 100 percent for the 16 profiled churches in this study. As noted in Thumma and Travis (2007), the comparable rate for predominately White megachurches is 34 percent. A similar pattern is evident concerning sermons about personal spiritual growth. Although sermons about social justice and racial issues are preached less often, relatively speaking, Black megachurches are more apt to be exposed to these subjects than their counterparts from smaller Black churches.

When music worship components are assessed in Table 2.1 (Panel 2), as suggested in other studies, a lower relative percentage of Black megachurches include spirituals during Sunday worship services. However, modern gospel music is more commonly used in larger Black churches than smaller ones. Similarly, a greater percentage of smaller

Black churches "never" use gospel rap music or dance and drama as compared to their larger counterparts. These figures illustrate both the continued importance of music in the Black Church tradition as well as the increased tendency by larger Black congregations to incorporate contemporary, secular-influenced music forms during worship. However, worship and teaching expressions are similar across the church size categories (Table 2.1, Panel 3). Sacred scripture is either "very" or "extremely" important in worship and teaching for over 92 percent of Black churches regardless of size. As expected, historical creeds are more common among smaller churches (72 percent) and decline in use with church size. The comparable rate for the national sample of White megachurches is 24 percent (Thumma and Travis 2007). Lastly, regardless of church size, emphasis on the Holy Spirit and personal experience are the norm for the Black congregations. These patterns illustrate how contemporary worship styles as well as historic Black Church worship components are part of worship and instruction—particularly for larger Black congregations.

Conclusion: Let Everything that Hath Breath

The Black megachurch socialization process begins upon entry into the sanctuary. Although the experience focuses on worship, it has multiple objectives. Scholarship on the megachurch in general contends that these congregations provide worship that emphasizes entertainment value. A similar argument might be made for Black megachurches that closely ascribe to a White evangelical worship style.[20] However, this tendency was not evident in this study. Quite the opposite, the vast majority of worship styles exhibited among the Black megachurches here are heavily influenced by historic Black Church worship elements and popular culture than White Evangelicalism. My assessments parallel commentary by Battle (2006): "the African American style of worship proves to be variegated and dynamic, and it must be concluded that African American people have indeed adopted a wide variety of styles of worship" (p. 92). I posit that much of what we are currently witnessing across Black megachurches is much less "new worship styles," but rather more extravagant, technologically savvy versions of the wide-ranging celebratory worship forms that make up the Black Church tradition. Furthermore, Black megachurches and their smaller Black counterparts share and swap worship elements. For example, call-and-response and gospel music can be found in the former worship services just as praise teams, praise dancers, and holy hip-hop are being incorporated by the latter.[21] And just as terminology such as "bling bling," "boodilicious," and "chillaxing"[22] from hip-hop and popular culture are now part of mainstream vernacular, concepts such as favor and "slain in the spirit" associated with the Black megachurch tradition are becoming more common among smaller Black congregations.

For certain Black megachurches here, particularly those with younger pastors and more recently built edifices, opulence is tied to excellence. Large sanctuaries, technological gadgetry, coffee shops, and praise dancers may seem ostentatious to outsiders, but are common features expected by members. Similarly, large-scale, well-choreographed worship services make sense logistically (i.e., a bigger choir results in the requisite volume for the venue and timely worship means multiple services can take place in a single day) and reflect the nature of a large church. Furthermore, continued exposure to larger than life worship and activities eventually become the experience that attendees anticipate. Worship includes numerous opportunities to challenge congregants to evoke their agency in non-traditional ways as members of God's elect. These same services condition congregants with tangible evidence of favor. One can imagine the potential effects as congregants are continually exposed to life-size statues of biblical figures; stained glass characterizations of Black matriarchs and patriarchs; acacia wood floors; multiple elevators similar to those found in office buildings; and, 40 foot steeples. Other images of *a more excellent way* include: 75-person usher board contingencies in tailored suits; ministerial staffs in color-coordinated attire; 150 members males choruses in Afrocentric attire; family life centers; barber shops; gymnasiums; ice-cream parlors; full-course Sunday breakfasts; and, senior pastors who know as much about foreign affairs, current events, and local politics as they do the Old Testament. I contend that these dynamics represent more than pomp and circumstance. They become a way of life. They reflect both a cultural context and a set of cultural expectations. Congregants hear a message of success in its many forms; they see it as well. And it becomes a common, consistent part of the church socialization process.

In these instances, worship moves beyond praise and becomes an instructional experience that is particularly salient for Blacks who work in structured, professional spaces and live lavishly (or at least comfortably) and consider their churches to be extensions of their personal and professional lifestyles. These same tangible and intangible dynamics are equally important for Blacks who are not exposed to such opulence on a daily basis. For them, weekly worship and other church activities provide exposure to things to which they aspire and are striving to acquire. Exposure to opulence and excellence become examples of what is possible with initiative and godly favor. Yet what may seem surprising to some readers is the actual *lack* of ostentatiousness among the vast majority of these Black megachurches, particularly older congregations and those pastored by older clergy. Although these churches are larger in size, they are absent many of the trimmings typically associated with televised megachurches. However, churches that are not overly ornate are still exceptionally immaculate in their furnishings and attention to detail. Pristine bathrooms, well-organized classrooms, and well-maintained properties are seemingly mundane features, but also subtly convey a message of success. Church staff is visible and on duty in order to maintain well-established spaces. And high-tech systems are in place to enhance worship and teaching programs. Like a "model home," rarely does anything appear "out of place." Equally evident in other programs and activities, this expectation of excellence is an extension of the understanding of what it means to be Christian *and* part of that spiritual community.

I contend that in the Black megachurch tradition, worship represents a time of collective instruction where a captive audience can be socialized toward the specific vision and theology of a charismatic senior pastor. Not only do congregants "see" physical examples of success on the church grounds, they are taught that God can make similar successes possible to the faithful and that they should expect them. Common discourse suggests that you can expect to prosper as your soul does. And when the praises go up the blessings come down—total praise—radical praise. According to most sample clergy, worship should be a grand experience because of the nature of God. A *big* God deserves *big* praise. A *great* God deserves *great* praise. Worship should mimic the impressive nature of God. Praise should be extreme because it is indicative of the extreme nature of the deity. Interestingly, this stance is reminiscent of the historic, sometimes troubling tendency of Black Christians to "bring their best to church" (i.e., by wearing their best attire, erecting an impressive edifice, and making sure the pastor and his family were well taken care of no matter how poor the congregation). And although worship reflects an extreme, multi-faceted expression of praise, it is still believed to be an insufficient response when one understands the nature of God. A similar type of instructional process may take place outside Black megachurch walls. However, the intentionality with which it is brought to bear through the use of long-held Black Church cultural tools and the most effective elements from other arenas results in a formidable church acculturation process.

Table 2.1 Black Church Worship Components by Church Size

	Average Sunday Attendance			
	Faith Factor Data			Current
	0–999	1,000–1,999	2,000+	Sample
Panel 1: Sermon Content				
Question: How often does the sermon focus on the following: (% Always)				
God's love and care	82.6	91.7	100.0	100.0
Practical advice	64.2	72.2	92.9	100.0
Personal spiritual growth	72.7	80.6	78.6	87.4
Social justice	25.7	33.3	42.9	87.4
Racial situations	17.6	16.7	42.9	50.0
Panel 2: Worship Music				
Question: During your congregation's regular worship services, how often are the following included as part of the service? (% Always or % Never)				
Spirituals ((% Always)	50.6	44.4	35.7	50.0
Gospel music (% Always)	27.4	33.3	64.3	100.0
Gospel rap music (% Never)	46.6	22.2	28.6	37.5
Dance or drama (% Never)	18.6	11.1	7.1	6.3
Panel 3: Worship and Teaching				
Question: How important are the following in the worship and teaching of your congregation? (% Very or Extremely Important)				
Sacred scripture	97.5	97.2	92.9	100.0
Historical creeds	72.1	52.8	64.3	25.0
Presence of Holy Spirit	98.7	100.0	100.0	100.0
Personal experience	87.2	91.7	85.7	87.4
n	1786	36	14	16

Faith Factor 2000 data: N=1,863. Black mega church sample: N=16. Note: Black megachurches from the Faith Factor 2000 data are identified in the third column as congre gations with average Sunday attendance of at least 2,000 persons. The fou rth colu mn reflects the churches from this stu dy. Refer to the appendix for addit ional su rvey questions and response options. The highest rates for each worship or teaching component are underlined.

Notes

1. Readers should compare and contrast this composite of the sample Black megachurch worship experience with that forwarded by Thumma and Travis (2007) about megachurches in general. The latter authors also present an informative typology of worship styles based on megachurch types that makes reference to the Black megachurch experience.

2. Consistent commemoration of the Lord's Supper and baptism contrasts with Thumma and Travis' (2007) findings about megachurches in general. In their 2007 megachurch study, they find that that only 40 percent of the sample of predominantly White megachurches "often" or "always" include the Lord's Supper in worship.

3. Billingsley (1999), Drake and Cayton (1940), Gilkes (2001), Higginbotham (1993),

Lincoln (1984), Lincoln and Mamiya (1990), Mays and Nicholson (1933), Morris (1984), West (1982), Wilmore (1994).

4. Lee (2005), Thumma and Travis (2007).

5. My observations deviate from Thumma and Travis (2007) who suggest that megachurch sermons focus on practical issues, but are largely conservative in their approach to issues. Similarly, Ostling and Hajratwala's (1991) op-ed account suggests that large churches grow by espousing a "conservative theology" (p. 2).

6. Refer to Wilson (1996) about the marriageable male dilemma. Black males are disproportionately represented among the incarcerated. The 2005 incarceration rate in state or federal prison and jail was 4,682 per 100,000 for Black males, 1,856 per 100,000 for Hispanic males, and 709 per 100,000 for White males. Among Black non-Hispanic males age 25 to 29 years, about 11.9 percent were in prison or jail as compared to 3.9 percent of Hispanic males and about 1.7 percent of White males in the same age category (Harrison and Beck 2006). Also see Fountain (2005) and West (1993). References to the "down low" were noted (King 2004) and other information about Black sexuality can be found in Davis (2005) and Neuman (2002).

7. Barnes and Jaret (2003) discuss housing dynamics. See West (1993) about issues of race and discrimination.

8. Edwards (2009), Lincoln and Mamiya (1990), Rivera (2002), Tucker-Worgs (2002).

9. Refer to artists such as Michael J. Smith ("Lord You Are Good") and Rich Mullen ("Our God Is an Awesome God"), and praise and worship songs by Maranatha! Praise Band and Tommy Combs. These songs were usually syncopated and gospelized, resulting in a different presentation from the originals.

10. Artists such as Kirk Franklin, Richard Smallwood, Corky Norwood, and as well as songs by mass and community choirs made popular during the 1980s and 1990s.

11. Similar efforts include "Passing the Peace" to shake each other's hands, welcome visitors, and speak to friends as well as being asked to introduce oneself to pew neighbors, hold their hands during prayer or hug them after the benediction. Even if persons do not remember names in these instances, they are more likely to recall "friendly" faces of persons who sat nearby or spoke to them during subsequent services and activities. A variety of such activities occur during a single worship service.

12. Dancers were elaborately dressed and provided dance presentations during certain periods of the service. However, at one AME church in New York, adult females rendered praise dances—adorned in red and white and waving scarves—throughout the entire service and during multiple services.

13. Barnes (2009), Dyson (1996), Kopano (2002), West (1993).

14. Event occurred summer 2007.

15. For information on the role of gospel rap to reach Black youth, refer to Ballard and Stewart (2006), Ehrlich (1997), LeBlanc (2001), Morthland (1997), and Simmons, McDaniels, and Linden (1993).

16. The acronym refers to Historically Black Colleges and Universities. Step teams are a central part of fraternity and sorority life on many Black college campuses.
17. Barnes (2009). It is also common for Black megachurches to provide sports teams, cheerleading squads, and bands. However, unlike similar secular activities, all interested children can participate in these church programs. Thus children and youth who might not be able to qualify or be selected for secular teams have opportunities to participate and receive recognition in supportive church settings.
18. Thumma and Travis (2007), Vaugh (1993).
19. Refer to the megachurch study performed by Thumma and Travis (2007).
20. Battle (2006) makes reference to three broad groups of Black churches, emotionalist (focuses on emotional and hysterical worship expressions), individualistic church (emulating White European American worship style); and, affirmationist congregations (affirms and celebrates authentic Black worship, ministry, and church life). The Black megachurches here are even more diverse than suggested by his three-part typology.
21. Refer to Edwards (2009) work that shows verbal affirmation among both Black and White churches.
22. Refer to Barnes (2009) about holy hip-hop in Black Church worship. "Chillaxing" is a combination of the words "chilling" and "relaxing."

Chapter Three

Church Socialization Processes

Each One, Teach Some!

THE CHAPTER SUBTITLE IS MORE than a play on words from a popular religious slogan, but I contend, inculcates mechanisms required for the efficient administration of Black megachurches. This chapter outlines some of the educational and instructional processes used by church leaders as well as methods that shape how leadership ultimately conveys its intentions to congregants. Getting things done in these large collectives does require steadfast support of a charismatic senior pastor. Yet he or she can be considered the central cog in a complex, expansive wheel that is understood to be collaborative. Meeting objectives also involves tapping into the considerable resources and know-how of clergy, lay leaders, and outside sources. This chapter broadly describes the church socialization process by considering how church cultural tools, practicalities, and specialized leadership training become intricately interwoven under the deft guidance of senior pastors to create spiritually driven management teams that often rival those found in large corporations. The chapter ends with case studies that detail two examples of systemic church transformations where pastors led processes that dramatically altered the nature of their respective church cultures—and the trials and triumphs that ensued.

Showing and Teaching Relevance

Pastors are clear and deliberate about the steps necessary to develop and convey their respective church missions. Interestingly, for most, building a megachurch was not initially their objective. Church growth was one of the outcomes of a well-planned church vision. They spoke of building a church that both paralleled the New Testament model and represented authentic reflections of their specific spiritual vocations. In addition to providing members with a clear church purpose and its spiritual impetus, part of the church socialization process involves communicating the relational dimensions of Christianity because the latter feature will shape how members negotiate society and commit to their respective congregations. Pastors are also challenged to socialize members to associate their personal beliefs with practical outcomes—including church volunteerism:

> [pastor's name] has sought to move the church congregation from just seeing church as someplace you come and sit, listen to the preacher preach and just go home—but he truly wants to take the living Word of God and make it practical in our lives. So we seek to take the scriptures and say, 'OK there is a relevancy of God's word in our everyday lives' and that's what really propels the ministry forward. (clergy representative from a Baptist church in the South)

These clerics believe that by making "the Word" relevant, congregants will be more likely to incorporate the bible in their everyday lives. Moreover, if the scripture is understandable and accessible, people will establish a deeper affinity for that source of instruction—the Black megachurch and pastor. And the specificity, intensity, and consistency with which pastors and other church leaders convey the church mission will determine how deeply engrained this information becomes in the lives of members. The same cleric continues:

> Kingdom theology [his church theology] suggests that God is intimately concerned with every aspect of our lives. So our strategic life plans are helping us develop not only spiritual goals, but also educational goals and goals for your family, economic goals, generational goals that will go beyond our lifetimes.

In order to help ensure appropriate socialization, church foci have a transparent nature. The overall church mission, reflected in scripture, must also move beyond its literal biblical meaning such that it becomes broadly applicable. Scholars such as Schaller (1990) point to relevance as a key factor in stimulating the megachurch phenomenon as congregations seek to meet a myriad of needs beyond the spiritual. I further suggest that relevance among Black megachurches takes on an additional dimension because it represents the space where one can learn what it means to be Christian, Black, a citizen, and victorious despite the odds. If accomplished correctly, members look to their respective congregations and pastors for answers despite the many societal arenas competing for that same influence—and despite the ever-present alternative to concede victory to deleterious structural forces.

Although other congregations may attempt a similar socialization process, I posit that what makes Black megachurch efforts unique and, in most cases, more effective, is a socialization method of melding cultural components from the most indelible aspects of both the Black Church tradition and Black history with extreme biblically justified expectations. Black megachurches also benefit from the historic place the Black Church has played in the lives of Blacks. This means that pastors who understand this "sacred connection" and maximize it are best positioned to influence the many facets of their congregants' lives as well as their church commitment. In addition to guiding the content of their educational messages, savvy pastors strive to maximize periods when they have the undivided attention of congregants:

> I think that the Church has to be concerned about liberating African Americans because the African American Church, for the most part, is the only place where Black people will gather consistently on a weekly basis. We have to use that weekly gathering to share with our people about the disparities in our school systems, the disparities in bank lending, the disparities in healthcare. And so for the Black pulpit to not become a liberating place would be less than a good use of that pulpit…there will be no community meeting that will have as many people as churches would have across the country. And so we have to use that time to also share the right information for our people. (pastor of a Baptist church in the Midwest)

This pastor expresses a clear belief about how he should use the pulpit beyond its original function as a place of religious instruction. A weekly captive audience engaged in what is largely a one-way "conversation" means preachers can present information, as well as reinforce it. And for him, a well-informed congregation can become a liberated one. According to the above clergy, much like a classroom, the space where Black Christians congregate weekly must be transformed into a seat of learning where the bible becomes the jumping-off point for exposing attendees to a myriad of other issues pastors believe should concern them. The next leader of a southern church affiliated with the United Church of Christ further expands this notion of relevance and intentionality by describing a *formula* to attract and instruct consumer savvy Christians:

> In March 1987, we met at a hotel and that's when [church's name] started. We went from 100 to 1,000 to 2,000. Up to a few years ago, we were approaching 7,500....It is location. If the demographics are right, it's no accident that most of your megachurches are in booming cities, Atlanta, Houston, Dallas, Phoenix, but most are located in that Sunbelt, Bible Belt because that's where the population has migrated and that's where you have many, many young professionals....Many young couples—people looking for a good place to establish themselves...and of course church is big in the southern tradition. So you get your job, you get your house, and you find yourself a good church...and then with the demographics you [referring to a church] have to have a program. You have to have ministries that speak to children's needs, teen ministries, support ministries for alcohol, drug addiction, you have to have support groups for married couples, activities for singles....It's programming combined with a dynamic worship—you got to have that music pumping. You got to speak directly to people and make people know that the Word is for them every Sunday. We're beyond the day when people just come to hear oratory. They come to hear a Gospel that is relevant to where they are...now I don't think people put as much emphasis on the articulation as they do what is this message saying. It's very utilitarian, user friendly-oriented now in our churches.

His assessment parallels some of the existing research on the internal and external factors needed to build a large church.[1] It also informs us that, although *place* can make a church attractive, what actually *takes place* there in terms of programs, activities, and planned worship—with an air of spontaneity—can render it almost indispensible in the minds of members. And formally educated worshipers expect education to be a part of their church experience. Although a neo-Pentecostal flair that was historically part of "mass" rather than "class" churches has supplanted stoic preaching from the latter tradition, attendees still expect "meat" rather than "milk." To a certain degree, people who feel entitled in the secular arena have become spiritually entitled Christians and expect their local church to respond accordingly. Knowing one's demographic means being able to develop user-friendly teaching/learning spaces that resonate with that market.[2] However, unlike their middle-class White megachurch counterparts, race-based gatekeeping and glass ceilings, single-parent families, wealth inequality, labor force inequities, educational gaps, as well as social problems even economically stable Blacks face bring them to the local church with an additional set of concerns and needs:

> So if you have a practical message that people can take home with them, put it in reach, you offer programs that speak to family needs and the struggles that people have with finances and how to get out of debt and how to attain your first mortgage, then people will gravitate toward that. And if you do that you [meaning the church] can grow by leaps and bounds. (pastor of a United Church of Christ congregation in the South)

Just as the self-help tradition was an integral part of the historic Black Church, I argue that this continues to be the case among Black megachurches. A larger segment of congregants may be middle and upper class, but they continue to look to their home church to help make their lives easier. However, self-help is not synonymous with handouts and the Black megachurch serves as a tangible example of what one can do if one is self-efficacious. The saying "God helps those who help themselves" takes on a new meaning in churches that, based on a belief in godly validation and ingenuity, represent success on a variety of fronts. This message is directly or indirectly ingrained in a wide variety of Black megachurch messages. It is also learned via exposure. More socioeconomically successful members require this type of environment and more economically strapped ones believe some of that favor and success will eventually rub off on them.

Scripture as the Foundation for Educational Success

The message of favor and expectation postulated by many Black megachurches would be hollow if it were not steeped in biblical justification. Members are taught to strive for spiritual maturity and, in some churches, material blessings because *God says* that is what Christians should anticipate. Other studies suggest that megachurches tend to espouse a conservative theology. That is generally not the case in this study sample. Yet, as expected, scripture serves as a primary cultural tool in the educational processes. The vast majority of churches here embrace a more prophetic understanding of scripture. Only one congregation can be considered biblically conservative:

> We lean more toward Fundamentalism...not to the extreme, but understand-
> ing the scriptures to be the Word of God and also being able to rightly divide
> ...know when it's God's Word and not just literature that's good to choose
> whether or not you want to follow—we believe this [points to the bible] is the
> Word of God, but not Fundamental to the point of being extremist or fanatic.
> (co-pastor of a Pentecostal church in the Midwest)

Although she emphasizes her church's traditional base, this cleric para-phrases 2 Timothy 2:15 to illustrate that their primary focus is to teach members how to accurately understand the bible without the extreme interpretations commonly associated with Fundamentalism. According to her next statement, a strong biblical basis is at the heart of a well-balanced Christian life: "if we can get the spiritual piece together, we might get the rest together....I think we [referring to Christians] are lacking a lot where the spiritual is concerned."

Pastors tie a traditionally priestly Black Church focus to outcomes that are often more prophetic by underscoring the necessity of scripture as the precursor for spiritual and personal empowerment.[3] Moreover, the process of "rightly dividing" scripture should result in spiritual growth. Just as Black megachurch members expect a great deal from their respec-tive congregations, leaders expect to see spiritual growth on the part of members in the form of, among other things, volunteerism, financial support, and successful Christian living.[4] The following co-pastor of a nondenominational church in the Midwest explains his church's social-ization process:

> Advancing spiritual maturity...once a person gets saved, we want him to
> grow up. We don't want them to remain baby Christians. We want them to get
> strong to the point where they are able to disciple someone else and to help

someone else grow. So we teach, my wife and I, teach messages that cause the individual Christian to grow spiritually and to mature spiritually...purpose fulfilling. We believe that and we teach that everyone is sent to this earth for a specific purpose, for a specific reason, and so our teaching guides people toward going to God and speaking to Him and praying to Him until they hear His plan for their life.

Thus the objective of church instruction is to get Christians on target with their lifelong godly vocations. The notion of a process of spiritual growth is a consistent theme—as is the role of the pastor, other clergy, and key lay leaders in directing that process. This same pastor believes that once Christians are actively engaged in God's ministry, material and physical blessings will result. However, he is critical of what he considers faulty biblical instruction that has caused Christians to miss opportunities to maximize their spiritual and material potential:

It's because of traditional religious teaching...probably the greatest influence on Christianity is the Catholic Church. And somewhere along the line the Catholic Church began to require priests to take vows of poverty, to demonstrate their humility. Now it's not scriptural, but it became a requirement. And I believe that out of that, it's pervasive now throughout Christianity....And so denominations are teaching, poverty equals holiness. No it doesn't. Have you read the Old Testament? Abraham, and he's the father of faith, and God says He's going to bless him and make him great and make his name great. And then you find out he became very wealthy and when you look at most of the Old Testament men of faith, there was no poverty in their life. There was no lack in their life. There was abundance in their life. They were able to help others and be generous to others.

Part of his church socialization process involves incorporating the experiences of biblical characters that help convey a particular message. As a Prosperity proponent, this theology undergirds every dimension of church life. Other religious traditions, denominationalism, or social problems that might undermine a message of spiritual and economic expectations are directly confronted and dispelled through concerted preaching and teaching. By deliberately linking the bible and characters from it to favorable outcomes most people wish to experience—the absence of poverty and sickness—such pastors are able to attract large followings as well as strengthen their stance among existing congregants.

Another Black Church cultural component used as an educational device is references to iconic figures from Black history. Clergy tap into a shared memory to make instructional messages more palatable by recollecting larger-than-life persons and events from periods when Blacks were victorious despite seemingly insurmountable odds. In contrast to the previously quoted pastors who ascribe to Fundamentalism and Prosperity theology, the next pastor's biblical basis includes a Social Gospel message that he has implemented to bring about inclusivity:

> Now we don't get anywhere as oppressed classes of people by setting ourselves up over and against other oppressed classes. Dr. King tried to tell us that and that's a lesson we have not learned yet. We have not learned that yet in the Black Church. I don't think we've learned that our condoning of sexism and homophobia in the Black Church contradicts the whole Civil Rights legacy of the Black Church. We don't see the contradiction. We don't understand that we as a people who have been victims of marginalization for years—and still are—turn around and without any conflict of conscious, condemn and isolate and dehumanize others. That has got to be challenged. And that's got to be challenged through systematic theology and through church administration and through prelates and administrative boards in higher places. (pastor of a UCC Church in the South)

For this pastor, challenging traditional ways of thinking meant entering into dialogue with his church members about controversial and often-sensitive topics. He has been able to incite congregational activism akin to the Black Church's social action in the 1960s by strategically referencing iconic people and events such as Dr. Martin Luther King Jr. and the Civil Rights Movement. His efforts to re-socialize his congregation are steeped in a Black Church prophetic tradition to fight "isms" as a consequence of the salvific message.

Despite theologies that can be considered priestly, prophetic, or somewhere in between, the pervasive and often creative use of scripture as a guiding force in preaching and teaching is evident. By quoting the biblical *address* from which their beliefs emanate and strategically proof texting to justify decisions, pastors possess the necessary validation to socialize their congregants as they do. However, of equal importance is their ability to effectively convey to the masses how God is specifically "speaking to them" from that same text. It is the effectiveness of this latter skill that often distinguishes many Black megachurch clergy from their peers in smaller Black congregations. Moreover, the ability to also find biblical relevance for challenges specific to the Black community separates them from their predominately White Church counterparts. They appear able to do so partly because of the tendency of Black Christians to continue to consider the bible the infallible Word of God. Although each sample cleric has a unique understanding about how scripture informs their overall church posture, several commonalities are evident including: the centrality of "the Book" in formal and informal church instructional spaces; scripture and larger-than-life biblical characters to justify extreme expectations on various fronts; emphasis on trials and triumphs from Black history in general; and, reliance on cultural tools from the historic Black Church tradition to create a shared memory that substantiates inevitable success despite circumstances.

Practical Approaches to Educational Success

No matter how important the biblical underpinnings of Black megachurch educational efforts are, they would be unsuccessful without practical, tangible guidance, and a strong, yet adaptive infrastructure to support them. So the bible provides the spiritual impetus for action, yet discerning Black megachurch leaders must take the next step in helping people make their spiritual dreams and aspirations a reality. Once congregants realize that God wants them to live abundant lives, they need to know how to accomplish this task. If the bible says that followers will prosper as their souls do, that God blesses virtuous women, that a well-trained child will live long, and that biblical characters such as Abraham and Solomon were successful both spiritually and materially, folks want to know how to make these things happen. It is here that the singular influence of cafeteria-style programs becomes most marked. Religious programs reinforce church stance and help congregants experience spiritual maturity—participation in such efforts also signal to church leadership that one is growing spiritually and deserving of God's favor as well as possible church leadership. Church-based secular programs also provide the nuts and bolts to actualize other blessings promised in scripture. According to the following pastor of a Holiness church in the Washington, D.C., area, varied educational programs help fulfill church and community needs:

> We're proud of the food bank, we're proud of the clothing bank. We have a tutorial program, where we help kids in the neighborhood with homework. We were one of the first churches to establish a GED program that grew into a full employment service...we actually provide job readiness, prepare them for work, show them how to fill out resumes and actually find jobs for people—so all of those are needs that are being fulfilled in the community....we have a computer lab there. And now we house, in addition to our school, we now lease space to a charter school....I wanted it to be a community center and that's what it is.

In addition to responding to issues of subsistence, the above pastor describes a litany of other practical training programs that indelibly tie his congregation to a poor urban space. Like this church and indicative of a linked fate understanding of the Black experience, it is common for the sample congregations to offer a variety of educational programs and community services, but also make their churches available to other local organizations. Another leader believes that his church's special calling involves helping the previously incarcerated transition back into society:

> So you [referring to his church] come outside of these walls and you tangibly demonstrate by a job training program and you don't care whether a person is saved or not—they can come right out of prison or right out of a rehab and you embrace them and show them that God has a plan for their life that transcends their past experience and a greater vision for them—you demonstrate tangibly. So that's what I believe we're here to do. (co-pastor of a nondenominational church in the Midwest)

The above pastor believes that the inspirational and practical activities his church provides represent an important stop gap in determining whether people are either irreparably set back or can bounce back from incarceration and poverty.

Making Christianity relevant is also evident as Black megachurches provide useful resources during accessible sermons that foster holistic living. Thus practical education takes place during programs, but also from the pulpit. During a Mother's Day sermon, "Let's Get Physical," one sample pastor illustrates the ability to skillfully broach the potentially sensitive subject of poor health in the Black community, in general, and Black women's weight, in particular, in a manner that challenges listeners without being caustic or condemning. After providing a personal testimony about how his health problems have been alleviated by a new health regimen, this pastor provides startling obesity statistics for Blacks, followed by a whimsical reinterpretation of a well-known biblical passage to reinforce his point in a nonconfrontational way:

> We may need to rewrite the 23 Psalms—My weight is my shepherd; I shall not want low calorie food. It maketh me munch on potato chips and bean dip; it leadeth me into 31 Flavors. It restoreth my weight: It leads me in the paths of cream puffs and bakeries, Yea though I waddle through the valley of Weight Watchers, I will fear the skim milk: for my appetite is with me; my Snickers, M&Ms, and Reese's cups comfort me. Thou annointest my body with calories; my scale tippeth over; my clothes runneth tighter: and I will dwell in the house of Little Debbie and snack cakes all the days of my life. (pastor of a Baptist church in Midwest)

Embedded in amusing banter is the biblical motivation for Black women to exercise and embrace being "nappy-headed holy" because "it's God's will that we get our health back." Quirky commentary is followed by more candid remarks:

> There is a relationship between Christianity and cholesterol. There is a relationship between spirituality and the spa....God has something for you to do and you can't do it if you don't have the health to do it...make the connection between being a Christian and being in good health....God wants to get some things done through you...[referring to unhealthy food and its effects]...it's cocaine, it's crack.

In addition to tapping into a collective pop culture recall of Olivia Newton John's Top 10 hit for his title, this practical sermon includes anecdotes, Physiology 101, and sobering medical findings interspersed with humor as it culminates into the challenge to "THINK THIN"—an acronym that reflects the pastor's healthy living/eating plan. Women are ultimately challenged to transform their *temples* in order to emulate Mary and her singular role as mother of Christ. Also reminiscent of a traditional teaching moment, a "fill in the blank" handout required congregational participation to reinforce the primary sermonic points. In light of the disproportionate health-related problems among Blacks, the resulting church-wide dietary changes the pastor attributes, in large part, to teaching events, illustrate the functional nature of educational moments in Black megachurches.

Quite possibly one of the most direct ways sample churches provide practical Christian socialization and instruction is through efforts to affect the lives of children and youth. Twelve of the 16 Black megachurches sponsor child care services; 50 percent provide organized academies or Day Schools. The general consensus is that if rigorous, intentional, bible-based educational programs are available for the young, churches can curtail the rates of teenage pregnancy, Black male incarceration, and poverty as well as the negative sociopsychological effects they can engender. Private schools enable Black megachurches to control the type and quality of information provided to students. As noted by the following pastor of a Pentecostal church in the Midwest, educational interventions are logical when one considers some of the less favorable alternatives; "when you have kids who are graduating who can barely read, we're sending them out into the community to become what? I don't know, but who's going to lead the city?" The imperative to organize Christian-based schools appears most evident among Black megachurches located in poor urban areas. For the following pastor, his vision to start a school was driven by subpar public schools as well as secular charter schools. He describes his church's Day School:

> The church has had some history in terms of dealing with pre-school education. But what I've tried to do is to take that foundation and expand it into something else that would have a larger impact....The smallest number of constituents that I have in the school, come from the church. (pastor of a Baptist Church in the Washington, D.C., area)

Interestingly, the above church's Day School provides an educational alternative for poor local families that indirectly serves as an evangelistic tool to the very same families because of its ability to meet a crucial need that the local government has been unable to provide. Furthermore, one of the benefits clergy suggest Christian private academies provide is wholesome responses to "street culture" that may be attractive to Black youth in general and young Black males in particular. As well as elevating the caliber of in-class instruction, this same pastor uses other opportunities to help youth become critical thinkers and understand the implications of doing so:

> I think that the most idiotic thing we've got going today is this whole notion of don't be a snitch. Our young people are growing up in an era where they think that it's important to keep your mouth shut. They believe that it is their duty to remain silent in the presence of that which is destructive....So every time I stand up and I'm talking to young people, I've got to tell them that there's another way, that there's another thought...to go beyond the idiocy of the moment.

Still another congregation attempts to initially attract urban youth by providing fun activities on the church site that potentially spur deeper interactions. By doing so, youth are minimally able to engage in activities such as basketball, bowling, tennis, and weight training in safe spaces; ideally, they begin to view the sponsoring church as a possible source to meet other needs:

> I was sitting here one day and I went outside and they'd just put the sign up across the street—for sale—that was an old, dilapidated warehouse and I was praying and the Lord said to me, 'You don't want the wrong people to move in there,' meaning, you need to buy that. I really wanted it to be a community center. So to attract the young people and especially the young boys, I said, 'we need some basketball hoops.' So they wouldn't let us put basketball hoops inside because of the beams that hold the building up. So I asked the city planners could we put a basketball court on the roof. So we have a basketball court up there. We have a tennis court up there. We're the only church with a computerized bowling alley in D.C. We have a four-lane bowling alley. All these are open to the community....Then we have a fitness center, where they come and exercise. We have a multipurpose room where community meetings can be held ...we also have a barbershop. (pastor of a Holiness church in the Washington, D.C., area)

According to this same pastor, the very practical nature of his church's cafeteria-style programs occurred as he listened to God's urging and made a tactical decision about how the space neighboring the church should be used. Although the impetus was spiritual, the project became viable through very real interactions with secular leaders and organizations. Additionally, the church has been able to help fight neighborhood social disorganization and establish ties with a group for whom it has been historically difficult to attract by responding to the interests of Black males.[5] Continuing education classes, bible certificate programs, and alliances with secular colleges that offer undergraduate and graduate degrees take place among the sample churches. One congregation operates an HBCU. The pastor of the latter institution describes their church's history of providing instruction in a historically Black setting:

> This Church started in 1926. Its first pastor was my grandfather who was a student at the oldest Black college in [name of state]. [Name] University was a university founded by slaves 4 months after the end of the Civil War in 1865. At the turn of the 19th century it was a preeminent example of Black self-help, Black self-determination. In fact, it was the only Black-owned university in the South that had a medical school, law school, and liberal arts college. It was a major Black university. (pastor of a Baptist church in the Midwest)

For him, the educational process is at its strongest when Blacks have the ability to determine the course of their instruction. By re-establishing an HBCU, his church provides one of the more extreme examples of the self-help legacy and linked fate ideology from the Black Church tradition. Furthermore, the relationship between this Black megachurch and the college is expected to bolster revitalization efforts and sidestep some of the economic challenges many HBCUs are facing today.[6]

Lastly, part of the formula for implementing practical programs requires churches to hold leaders and participants accountable for their involvement. Even the most well-run Black megachurch must assess program successes, responsiveness, and failures. The next representative quote echoes a common sentiment among clergy that goals for high expectations must be monitored using measurable outcomes. He provides an example specific to assistance, training, and placement services:

> Giving an overall view, I'll start with our employment ministry....We're able to see how many come through the job fair, how many people actually interviewed, how many were actually placed on a job...we actually get that type of

feedback from employers. Regarding financial or housing assistance...our instructors let us know, 'you referred ten members to the class, seven members came through and completed the class' so we're able to keep records that way as well. (clergy representative from a Baptist church in the South)

In addition to spearheading programs, administrators in the above church are responsible for assessing their effectiveness using tangible outcomes. Similarly, leaders hold participants accountable for becoming more self-efficacious as a result of their involvement. Doing things "decently and in order" takes on more than its initial scriptural meaning when one considers what is needed to organize, maintain, critique, and enhance cafeteria-style programs. For each Black megachurch, very practical approaches are implemented to expose congregants to the church's purpose and programs. The process is evident during worship and formal teaching activities such as Sunday school. But for certain people, particularly community members with problems, the process begins by meeting subsistence needs. Other activities involve demographic analyses to determine additional needs and interests of congregants and community members and responding both deliberately and according to the pastor's sentiments. Traditional educational opportunities such as schools exist, but some of the more creative teaching/learning endeavors such as semester-long job training courses, youth rite of passage programs, workshops to overcome sexual victimization, anger management classes, scouting programs for children with incarcerated parents, worship and training courses in Spanish, and youth evangelical training seminars represent attempts to take teaching and learning to another level.

Formal Approaches to Educational Success

Over 50 years after the landmark *Brown v. Board of Education* (1954) decision, Black children, particularly those who live in urban spaces, continue to lag behind their White counterparts in achievement levels. Yet they exceed this same group in terms of under-education and dropout rates.[7] Increasing numbers of Black parents are looking to charter schools, magnet schools, and private Christian academies to fill the void they perceive in public school systems.[8] According to the *Journal of Blacks in Higher Education* (2000–1), approximately 250,000 students are enrolled in charter schools; about 53,926 are Black. Other sources suggest over 2,400 charter schools serving over half a million students (Center for Education Reform 2001). Detractors accuse such schools of engaging in segregation and "creaming" the best public school students. Supporters describe positive, nurturing, "Ritalin-free," academically rigorous spaces where Black children can learn and are expected to do so.[9] Although limited data preclude definitive conclusions about the benefits of charter schools,[10] their reputations are growing for a variety of reasons:

> Clearly, there is strong political backing for charter schools across the nation, much more so than for vouchers for private school education at taxpayer expense. For many African American parents with school-age children, charter schools offer strong hope that their children will receive a quality K–12 education that will enable them to gain entrance to college and succeed in life. Many of these Black parents see promises of improvements in the public school system as too little, too late. Most African Americans are unwilling to wait for the politicians to get around to fixing the public schools. (*Journal of Blacks in Higher Education* 2000–1: 74)

And still others contend that these types of academic alternatives are largely efforts by both Whites to evade the consequences of desegregation or middle-class parents to avoid classrooms where their children will have to rub shoulders with poor and working-class peers. When magnet schools are considered, studies show they enroll about 1.2 million students and are usually located in large, urban areas.[11] And similar suspicions have arisen when magnet programs have been presented as a method to entice White suburbanites back into urban spaces. Whites remain reticent, wedded to their racial stereotypes and fears, while Blacks express disdain that such efforts amount to "running after" Whites.[12] According to Archbald (2004):

> There has been no shortage of articles and books on the potential of magnet schools, charter schools, or other forms of school choice to exacerbate economic segregation in public schools and curtail opportunities for economically disadvantaged children. (P. 286)

In *Another Kind of Public Education*, Collins (2009) provides a broad strategy of action in response to the current state of public education and democracy—for youth and adults alike:

> What the United States needs is another kind of public education—one that encourages us to become an involved, informed public. What this country needs is a recommitment to schools and other social institutions whose mandate lies in delivering the kind of public education that will equip us for this task. We miseducate the public and students when we dumb down big ideas....The charter school movement in Washington, D.C., Philadelphia, Los Angeles, and other urban centers may be an indication of this deep-seated disappointment with public schools. If urban public schools cannot seem to educate African American and Latino youth, many parents and community activists feel they can do better. If public institutions do not care about African American and Latino children, why shouldn't parents and leaders create private alternatives to public schools? (Pp. ix, 26–7)

Banks (2001) continues in a similar manner by suggesting a specific process:

> A transformative curriculum designed to empower students, especially from victimized and marginalized groups, must help students develop the knowledge and skills needed to critically examine the current political and economic structure and the myths and ideologies used to justify it...must teach students critical thinking skills...to view the human experience from the perspective of a range of cultural, ethnic, and social-class groups, and to construct their own versions of the past, present, and future. (Pp. 203–4)

These types of observations increasingly suggest that quality education must reflect cross-cultural competencies that help students understand and appreciate their identities and culture, as well as promote inclusivity, democracy, and citizenship. Despite the continued debate, private institutions wield considerably more power than public school systems to determine the nature and scope of their programs. Moreover, many intentionally serve low-income, bilingual, and special needs students.[13]

Despite a history fraught with blatant as well as much more covert exclusionary practices, the general consensus among research on education is summarized by Hallinan (2001); "school is a likely vehicle for social transformation" (p. 56). But his statement should be couched to consider both the potential benefits and drawbacks of organized education:

> Education constitutes a crucially important social institution in American society. On the one hand, it is a premier institution through which dominant interpretations are passed on from generation to generation. We all know that textbooks express the point of view of those who write and publish the books. On the other hand, educational institutions strive to cultivate the values and habits of democracy. Schools are frontline institutions for putting teeth into democratic possibilities in the U.S. context. (Collins 2009: 10–1)

If the "Catholic school advantage" is true,[14] Black megachurch-sponsored schools could fill an academic void if they reflect a climate with "strong academic curriculum, communal organization, decentralized governance, and an inspirational ideology in promoting students' engagement and academic achievement" (Hallinan 2001: 60). Interestingly, this same author describes other public school reform germane to the current study such as; "school choice plans; and the establishment of charter schools, magnet schools, alternative schools, and *all-Black academies* [emphasis is mine]" (p. 61).

Research is clear that three factors—students' personal drive and initiative, family closeness and family socialization processes, and supportive institutions such as schools—play marked roles in fostering the educational pursuits of children from poor families.[15] Furthermore, faith-based schools are responding in growing numbers to meet the third demand by "providing a space…where participants could comfortably and passionately practice and perform their faith through multiple texts and feel closer to God" (Eakle 2007: 504–5). In addition to establishing biblically based curriculum and programs, private Christian schools often provide the increased accountability required to prepare students for college. Furthermore, by creating environments—led by Black administrators and faculty, especially Black males—that acknowledge and celebrate both Christian *and* Black culture, such schools carve out a niche for themselves in the growing mosaic that is the private school system. In the tradition of modeling success, Day Schools, private academies, after care, day care, and their derivatives represent extensions of overall Black megachurch culture. This means that they must be stellar in terms of environment, curriculum, and programs. Table 3.1 summarizes the schools sponsored by the Black megachurches in this study.[16]

Leadership Training and Expectations

The leadership team of the profiled Black megachurches consists of a senior pastor (or co-pastors) surrounded by a network of paid and volunteer clergy and lay leaders responsible for day-to-day logistics. The size of the staff is correlated with church size and the number and type of programs offered. Although major decisions are not made without the senior pastor's approval, cults of personality do not appear to be the norm.[17] To the contrary, pastors seem to strive to train competent leaders and then empower them to make sound decisions. Pastoral responsibilities generally preclude micro-managing. Yet clergy and lay leaders who have been properly socialized become suitable *pastoral proxies* in their respective leadership roles and decision-making abilities. Responsibilities are multifaceted because leaders tend to have both spiritual and administrative roles. And it is crucial that they espouse and can succinctly articulate the church's stance and pastor's vision. Although Black megachurches may have a large number of clergy who are members, this does not mean they are automatically tapped for leadership. Those who serve as leaders must complete a rigorous vetting process that typically includes formal education, internal church training, and recommendations from other well-respected church leaders who are part of the pastor's inner circle. The following cleric at a church in the South describes his training experience:

> I joined [church name] in 1990. Around 1994, the church ministry, membership wise, exploded. So [pastor's name] sought to bring on more elders or ministers on staff. I was actually recommended by one of the other elders. So I was interviewed to be the Elder of Pastoral Care at that time. So I went through the interview process, [pastor's name] hired me and I was charged with actually putting together the entire Pastoral Care Ministry.

Highly credentialed in his own right, this minister could pastor a congregation. He does not formally preach during worship services, but is responsible for a substantial ministry and spoke with great pride about his calling at this specific church. His pastor has earned both a Doctor of Ministry and a secular degree. Formal education is a necessary but insufficient condition for leadership in light of the extensive internal training leadership candidates must also complete:

We are trained on site. Some of the elders have gone to seminary, some have gone to bible college, and then we do have our internal ministers in training and elders in training where there are formal classes that you need to go through before you become licensed or ordained.

The above church employs over 200 persons. Clergy leaders and top lay leaders hold unique positions based on their ability to model the pastor's stance and church mission.[18] Paralleling Harrison's (2005) case study of one Black megachurch, leadership accountability among these profiled churches is central. In general, acceptable leaders must have the requisite formal education and/or training; consistently volunteer and attend church programs; regularly attend Sunday school and bible studies; be able to convey their support for the church purpose, programs, and pastor; and consistently contribute tithes and offerings. Using technology that allows for on-line banking and bill payments in secular society, several congregations also strongly recommend that leaders and congregants arrange for their tithes to be automatically deducted from their bank accounts. These types of markers help confirm one's appropriateness as a church leader.

Although leaders, particularly those over large ministries or in critical roles, are often hand-picked by the senior pastor, the following pastor of an urban Holiness church in the Washington, D.C., area describes a contrasting, arduous process of initially cultivating adequate leadership:

You work with what He gives you. He didn't give us a church full of doctors and lawyers. We have them now, but I started with seven people in a storefront. And I had no idea at the age of 19, when I started the ministry, I'd have 7,000 members on roll. That was far beyond me. But He gave me the compassion and it was slow growth, but it was sure growth. And part of the ministry, many of the officers who serve here as deacons, trustees, deaconess, came from either drug abuse, alcoholism, some type of sexual promiscuous lifestyle and now they've been cleaned up, converted, and they help me run the ministry....He is sending us physicians, doctors now, but that's not how we were founded. We were just poor, Holiness, Pentecostal, sanctified people. Now we have arisen. And we're now recognized in the city as the largest Pentecostal church in [city name].

For this pastor, developing leaders meant recognizing the potential found in people who might ordinarily be overlooked for leadership in more middle-class congregations. He also suggests that these decisions make sense based on the assumption that each person has been sent by God to perform ministry. Moreover, this statement illustrates the considerable pastoral discretion indicative of the Black Church tradition (particularly among Baptists and independent churches) where pastors can make broad leadership decisions, arrange for church resources to subsidize leader training, and provide intra-church instruction. Lastly, the substantial growth among both the leaders and members of this Holiness church stand in stark contrast to the commentary captured by McRoberts (2003) and leveled by a pastor of a small Holiness church that "no pastor, in his view, could grow a church to gigantic proportions by preaching the steep price of salvation" (p. 63). The same pastor argues, "something is *wrong* [emphasis is his] if a Holiness church is too large on an ordinary Sunday" (p. 64). His comments seem short-sighted to sample clergy who believe that being *in the world, but not of it* does not preclude substantial church growth or other forms of prosperity.

Those churches that emphasize Afrocentricity make additional efforts to socialize leaders about Black history. Although it is logical that persons with similar personal politics would gravitate toward such churches, these pastors have strict requirements and accountability that clergy are trained to preach and teach from a Black-centered perspective using literature informed by the Black experience:

> [Name of church] focuses on theological education. When I was in school, I decided that if I ever got in a position to help somebody, I would do more than shake their hand and say, 'God bless you. I'm praying for you.' So we give more than $6,500 a year to students in seminary and have ordained 40 seminary graduates. You can't be ordained, in fact, at our church unless you are a seminary graduate. We have 58 students in seminary and we're paying for them—you have to be a member of this church and you've got to be active in the ministry. (pastor of a UCC church in the Midwest)

By subsidizing their formal training, he guarantees that his ministerial staff espouses the desired perspective. Furthermore, financial support can engender seminary graduates to their patron congregations in a way that builds unwavering commitment to both church and pastor. The same pastor explains the impetus for his church's training process:

> It was started because my first seminary graduate, ordained under my watch was a South African woman named [her name]. She graduated from seminary and hadn't read one Black book by nobody about nobody, but she was at a White seminary. So I said, if you go to Virginia Union, Howard, ITC, I know they will make you read something Black…I tell you, no other student will come out of this church without having read books by Black people and or about Blacks. So I started a program in '75 for that reason and it's that training, where they're reading Dwight Hoffman, Linda Thomas, Allan Callahan, and Cone—that gives them a vision for what ministry is….Thomas Hoyt, professor of New Testament said, 'Aint' nothing wrong with gravy, but anybody who cooks can tell you the best gravy is the gravy that oozes out the meat—give the folks some meat. We're not knocking preaching. You should be the best preacher you can be but, the church is a whole lot more than just preaching.

According to this cleric, it is egregious for Black clergy who are responsible for a predominately Black populace to fail to receive instruction in this regard. He does not appear to require clergy training to only reflect an Afrocentric approach, but that it must be principle. Matriculating at predominately Black seminaries and bible colleges will help insure that this objective is met. Furthermore, his reference to I Corinthians 3:1–3 concerning spiritual "meat" is a common theme as clergy describe the process by which church leaders, particularly ministers, are trained and expected to subsequently socialize the larger congregation. This same pastor concludes by justifying what may seem to be extreme educational stipulations for clergy. His observation applies to clergy in general and pastors in particular:

> They [referring to members] associate us with the holy of holy—good or bad. We represent God…she [referencing members] can't get to God, but she can get to you…I can't get to God, but let me see what Rev. says.

As might be expected, pastors' profiles help shape how they understand the socialization process. In general, pastors with more formal training require a similar level of training for ordination candidates. Lay leaders who wish to hold key positions often need to be similarly educated and attempts are made to match their background with designated church positions. In addition, it is common for clergy leaders to also have earned secular degrees in areas such as business, medicine, accounting, teaching, law, nursing, and social work. Once trained, they too are often matched to programs or ministries that parallel their areas of expertise. Yet all leaders are expected to be capable of conveying the spiritual message and mission of the church. In addition, those who are members of hierarchical denominations usually have additional requirements. When describing his decision to change denominational affiliation from Baptist to United Church of Christ, one pastor provides the following explanation:

> Why UCC? The UCC has a history of being the first to take risks on behalf of marginalized people. As I looked at the history of the UCC I saw that it went all the back to the Amistad incident of the 1800s. It went from there to Women's Rights and women's suffrage. The Social Gospel Movement of the early 1900s, dealing with the working conditions primarily of White working-class people, but still, the UCC was a voice for the rights of workers in terms of wages, in terms of working hours, even in terms of children being abused in the workplace. The UCC has done tremendous research in all of those areas and every ethical stance regarding social issues that the UCC takes is well researched and documented. I mean there are volumes of articles and research…in the Justice and Witness Ministry. I have not known of a denomination that held social justice in such esteem that it would actually devote resources, I mean personnel, a whole department, just to researching and promoting social justice issues. To me, that's more than just talking a good game, that's really walking the walk. And honestly, I have not found in any of the Baptist denominations that kind of commitment. It's not to say it's not there, but at the time, I was not really aware of it. And I also knew that particularly in regard to the issue of inclusion of gays and lesbians, as far as I know, not one of the Baptist Conventions, including the Progressives, are very progressive on that issue. (pastor of a UCC church in the South)

He references past accusations of anti-intellectualism, particularly among Baptist churches, as one of the factors that precipitated his denominational exodus. The social justice emphasis of the UCC resonated with his own beliefs and his vision as church leader. He is critical of the inconsistent nature in which White Christians have historically pursued social justice, but believes the UCC's educational model provides a sound *theoretical* basis for his own understanding of how inclusivity, community, and relationships should manifest in the church.

Seminary studies show that one can assess the strength of a given congregation, not by the number of attendees during worship services, but by the caliber of their Christian Education program.[19] Spiritually *strong* churches will have well-established, well-attended teaching/learning endeavors. The importance of Christian Education is apparent as clergy describe the requisite formal and intra-church training for leaders. It would appear that part of these lengthy processes serves to weed out less committed candidates as well as identify persons genuinely interested in learning and leading. Moreover, by establishing substantial training requirements, Black megachurch pastors ensure that leaders can espouse the church's stance, convey it coherently, and effectively represent the church in diverse settings. And because many of these leaders will be responsible for the church's cafeteria-style programs, it is all the more imperative that pastors trust that they are well trained to lead *and* to model the success for which they desire their congregations to be recognized.

Two Case Studies of Church Transformations through Re-Socialization

Case 1: Developing a Succession Plan

One of the most formidable challenges megachurches face in general is linked to leadership transition.[20] The substantial influence of the senior pastor has been illustrated in prior chapters. He or she drives church growth and programmatic efforts. However, when a church's identity becomes so heavily intertwined with the pastor's identity, it faces dilemmas if the senior pastor is no longer willing or able to serve. Problems surrounding succession have literally divided even the most well-organized congregations. Despite the implications of the subject and their generally well-organized churches, few pastors in this project discussed issues of succession. However, those who broached the subject help inform our understanding about another crucial socializing and educational process that involves proactively establishing a robust leadership framework and program agenda that can be implemented regardless of who is at the pastoral helm.

This developmental approach is insightful as an instructional device because succession plans require most churches to start at "square one" and map their church's future. What can make the procedure particularly unpleasant and laborious is that it involves making plans that, for all intents and purposes, do not include the senior pastor. And for some leaders and members, such a thought is unfathomable. Moreover succession plans require those involved to proactively think "outside the box" about often vague and nebulous issues that could potentially influence the nature of their church and its presence in the community. Examining some of the steps, milestones, and setbacks of the following case of a UCC Church in the Midwest provides a retrospective on how one congregation created a space that ultimately established its Black megachurch status and solidified its purpose for the future. In order to develop a broad church plan, the pastor initially began by challenging existing leaders to include and empower younger leaders during the process:

> In 2000, we had an evaluation retreat to determine what is working, what isn't. What could we do better? What did we learn from our failures? From our successes. At the end of the retreat, they started talking about the next twenty years. I said, 'we're stopping this retreat right here.' They said, 'Well Rev., we have to…' and I said, 'We don't have to do anything. Look around this table. There's nobody here but [name of the youngest participant] who will be here twenty years from now. We need to get kids *her age, like we were* [emphasis his] twenty years ago to put together their vision for the church.' And we did. About 20 persons, 15–40 years old, and five of us old people hung around for continuity and *they* put together the strategic plan for the next two years…so ministries are determined by what we put together in terms of our vision statement for the church, purpose, and the strategic plan.

The above steps resulted in a template from which existing and potential programs and activities are assessed for appropriateness and viability. It also undergirded a process to establish long-term church goals:

> So in that long-range ministry, we were looking at how we were growing, looking at what God is doing. I need to say this to help you understand how

powerful it was both in terms of God's spirit moving and to help you understand why and how we began to frame these questions that make us not pastor-focused...when we started the long-range planning ministry. After one devotion I said, 'Here's what I want you to do. I want you to take a piece of paper and pen and separate. Don't talk to anyone but God. Husbands and wives can't talk to each other, go back to a quiet place. I want you to ask God what you see for your church 5 years from now, 10 years from now, 15, and 20 years from now.'

Despite a clear pragmatic, administrative quality, his comment conveys the spiritual basis of the process where God is believed to instruct them collectively and the pastor challenged them individually to seek divine guidance. A critical element of the procedure is the intentionality required to insure that the church's mission was not pastor-focused, but rather God-focused. The collaborative method of such long-range planning calls into question long-held stereotypes about the top-down, dictator-like leadership styles associated with Black churches in general and with Black megachurches in particular. The pastor continues by describing a broader model informed by the Black tradition that also guided long-range planning:

There were 37 items on the lists from 27 people and then we began to prioritize and that's when the congregation made the Long-Range Ministry an official body of the church so this could go on. Because churches don't plan to fail. They fail to plan, they have no plan. One of the questions was, 'How do you build an institution, a Black institution, that's going to last? Where are all the Black institutions?' Freedoms Journal...banks are gone. What happened? What can we learn from them? And in looking at those institutions and looking at our institution, two things we began to do as early as '79, '80,' 81 was, OK, how do you build an institution that's built around the *personality of Jesus Christ* [emphasis is his] so that no matter who's at the head, the church is going on. How do you do that? And looking at that hard and coming up with some clear paths....Secondly, 'How do we organize a succession plan?' We said that in '79–'80, but nobody was paying attention to it until I turned 60. Then they said, 'you're getting to the age where we need to have something in writing.'

The model of an all-knowing, perfect Christ stands at the center of the church's succession plans and helps make seemingly extreme goals and objectives seem more achievable. This means that, like Jesus, the essence of the paradigm is social justice-oriented, considered radical for the times, love-centered, and sacrificial in its outcomes. This pastor is striving to make the church self-reliant by exposing congregants to different ministers, reminding them of their membership in God's church (not the pastor's), and purposefully training leaders to continue in his absence. Part of the pastor's challenge meant preventing leaders from becoming complacent based on *his viability* or their inability to imagine a time when he might not be viable, as well as understanding that success can include expectation of godly favor, but must include proactive efforts:

> As we looked at how to build an institution, one of the things we looked at was the financial piece. How do these Jewish churches and Catholic churches do what they do? They have an endowment. So we started an endowment so that—one of the long range goals was by 2015, every penny lifted in the offering would go to missions to Africa or the third world. How do you do that? With an endowment. Right now it's up to about 18 million that can't be touched …you can live on the interest. So that when we talk about ministry in Darfur, ministry in Cape Town, this is what the offering is for, helping somebody else. So we don't have to worry—'we need another $20 to pay the light bill, to pay the organist.' No. No. No. That's one of the practical things. Let's put in place a financial piece that will insure the ongoing of this institution so we're not living hand to mouth. Because a lot of Black churches live hand to mouth, payday to payday. We're trying to teach our people not to live payday to payday, let's institutionalize that as a church.

Another more practical aspect of the re-socialization process involved recognizing the business dimensions of the church by implementing an economic model to establish revenue streams and intentionally develop seemingly extreme mission efforts indicative of a Social Gospel message. Unlike Lincoln and Mamiya's (1990) description of the tensions associated with Black Church dialectics, by recognizing its multi-faceted, multi-functioning nature, this church has established an infrastructure that strives to optimize its charismatic *and* bureaucratic dimensions. The pastor's goal was to engage in a democratic exchange informed by information and resources inside and outside the congregation to create an economically stable church with relevant programs and leaders qualified and confident to serve in his absence. Furthermore, by mentoring young leaders, he is able to build their leadership capacities as well as ensure that the Afrocentric basis of the congregation continues into the next generation. Leaders, in turn, will convey this message to congregants—and the church's traditions will continue.

Case Study 2: Cultivating Affirming Spaces

Another church's re-socialization and re-education process was much more concertedly led by the pastor. He sought to radically alter the very nature of how congregants understand how inclusivity is connected to the relational dimensions of Christianity. The case of a UCC church in the South with a Baptist history illustrates: the results of considerable pastoral influence; the possibilities transformative instruction can cause; and, some of the extreme expectations Black megachurches can espouse. I also contend that understanding this church's experience sheds light on the reality of some of the pushes and pulls Black megachurch leaders can experience as they attempt to harness support for their visions from the masses. The church's re-education process actually began when the pastor began to question his own beliefs and the over-simplified views about Christianity instilled in him from childhood:

> I kind of went through stages. Actually I was one of those homophobic preachers that I now like to engage. It was because it was a part of my tradition. I was actually raised in a more conservative church….I was raised COGIC…In that upbringing—there's right, there's wrong, there's Black, there's White, there's good, there's evil, there's sin, there's righteousness. And you draw the line and you hold that line and you do not waver one iota. Because we were taught that holiness is not going to come down to you—you've got to come up to holiness. So I was raised in a religious setting where it was constantly drummed into us that you must meet the standard of righteousness. To be sure it was a 'works-righteousness' theology—I didn't realize it at the time but we were really proving ourselves worthy enough to be called the children of God by all the things we *refrain* from [emphasis is his]—playing ball on Sunday, drinking root beer because it had the word "beer" in it, alcohol, going to a party, all of that.

The re-socialization process meant breaking traditions correlated with two less-positive dimensions of Black Church culture—homophobia and heterosexism. The pastor rejected a dichotomous understanding of humanity's "sin-nature," and embraced a more nuanced model for Christian living that reshaped the church's theology, leadership structure, and views about what constitutes worthiness for full inclusion in the Christian community. Although he successfully grew the church to a membership of 7,000 persons, as his exposure to other theological perspectives increased, this pastor began to question its conservative stance. As his vision changed, so did that of his congregation:

> I began tentatively at first. I began to just be more aware of the Social Gospel dimensions in my sermons, whereas to just preach the Parable of the Good Samaritan as just everybody ought to help somebody, just do what you can to help your neighbor—I began to really explore the meaning of *neighbor* [emphasis is his] as someone who does not live beside you and in that particular parable, someone who does not believe what you believe. The Samaritans and the Jews had no dealings. And then to explore what that meant in light of what Jesus called us to do. Go and don't be like the Levite or the priest. Go and do like the Samaritan. So I began to reclaim and explore the Social Gospel dimension of everything that I was preaching and it kind of raised a few eyes. Some people said, 'Mmm, pastor is getting more political now' but they could live with that. You know, Dr. King OK, Civil Rights, OK, we can go with that.

He began to expose the membership to a Social Gospel message via preaching and teaching. New Testament passages such as Luke 10 that stress cultural tolerance and proactively developing inter-group relationships were used to justify inclusivity. Members were initially amenable because they associated his *new* messages with social action in the spirit of the Civil Rights Movement. The next transformative phase involved pushing the theological envelope by challenging sexism in the church:

> And then I took it a step further by saying that, if we really are going to be about the Gospel of Jesus, who was no respecter of persons in terms of person's gender, then it seems to me that we need to actualize that in our own church administration. So this time when we start talking about setting aside deacons, I do not want women to be excluded. We will have *women deacons—not deaconesses, not deacon's assistants, deacons* [emphasis is his]. Because a deacon is a servant. And there were a few who left over that, a few who just said, 'Now that's not Baptist. We can't do that because the church is the place where men assert their authority and we want to see men up front and we don't want women, because men are beaten down everywhere else. We got to see them up front and the deacons are for men.' [They asked] 'Why didn't Jesus call any women?' and I said, 'Well, He did, they just weren't one of the 12, but He called several women.' Well, naw, naw. So we went through all that. They were doing

it based on biblical and social reasons. There were some who felt that the
church is the last bastion for men to assert their manhood. And I said, 'What
you're saying is that the church ought to sanction patriarchy. The church ought
to sanction misogyny. And that can't be right.' And so a few said, 'No, we
believe in equality, but not equality between men and women, they aren't the
same. And if women want to serve, they can be missionaries. They can be dea-
conesses. They can be married to deacons, but not a deacon, not in the Baptist
Church.' There were some women who felt that way too. Matter of fact there
was one woman who challenged me on that and said, 'I'm just not comfortable
with that and the bible clearly says all of the 7 deacons were men.' And I said,
'Well then all of them have to be Jews too.' So I begin to really challenge people about this. And a few left. So a little ripple there.

According to the pastor, each instructional phase was biblically-informed
and linked to a model of a selfless Christ. He attempted to make the bible
more relevant and the proposed changes transparent such that his radical challenges to denominationalism, patriarchy, and homophobia
reflected *instruction through conversation*. As he challenged his own long-
held beliefs, he in turn, challenged the congregation's. Some members
countered with their own biblical interpretations, but his position as pastor as well as logical rebuttals and responses initially appeased most
naysayers. Despite sexism among males and hegemony among females,
most members were supportive of his bid against sexism. However, his
final decision to establish inclusive church spaces regardless of race,
class, gender, or sexual orientation was less favorably received:

> So I'm going to press the envelope a little further now by saying, 'In addition
> to equality between men and women, we ought to be breaking down the
> homophobic barriers that divide people along the lines of sexual orientation.'

He then describes a tumultuous crisis that ensued that resulted in the
exodus of half the congregation. Yet he points to godly validation and
clergy-congregant communication for maintaining his church base:

> And God is to be praised. God gets all the credit. But I was able to remain stead-
> fast in that conviction and invite people into dialogue. One of the things that
> crisis did was help me to invite people into dialogue about the meaning of the
> text [the bible] and the meaning of our witness as we interpret the text as peo-
> ple of God in our contemporary times. And so we've had discussions that we
> never would have had prior to that about sexuality, about sex, and it has

opened the door for fathers to talk to their own sons and wives to talk to their husbands and husbands to talk to their wives. And for us to really understand what being *a family of God* [his emphasis] is all about.

Despite substantial membership fallout, the above experience illustrates how leadership can expose members to potentially polarizing subjects and ultimately alter how many persons frame these issues. This pastor believes that open, honest dialogue has helped create more welcoming church spaces. Readers will notice that the two case studies focus on Black congregations associated with the United Church of Christ—a tradition considered more progressive than most. Both pastors describe an arduous process with beneficial end results. However, the latter church experienced a substantial decline in church membership as a result of the re-socialization process. Whether one considers the latter church's glass "half empty or full," both instances uncover the possibilities associated with creating spaces where leaders and members are empowered and equipped to move their churches into unchartered territories believed to be more relevant and visionary. The two cases also illustrate how even Black megachurches can experience growing pains and obstacles when contemporary church culture comes into opposition with other long-standing cultural traditions.

Conclusion

No matter their educational or experiential profile, Black megachurch pastors cannot do it all—those in the current study do not appear to want to either. They stand at the helm of a leadership network responsible for day-to-day logistics as well as accurately conveying the pastor's vision for the church to congregants and the community. Clergy responses suggest that the overall objective is to cultivate a congregation of well-informed members who can emulate the life and legacy of Jesus Christ as understood and conveyed by the pastor. To a certain degree, the instructional process described here parallels those found in other congregations. However, I posit that the broad socialization structure found among many Black megachurches tends to be much more strategic, intentional, multi-faceted, and adaptable to a multitude of objectives. Moreover, properly trained clergy and lay leaders are poised to educate and instruct laypersons by word and deed. And the latter method appears to be a frequently used and effective approach. The process also reflects education shaped by extremes that encompass: expectations; collective and individual larger-than-life objectives; zealous giving and volunteerism; and most of all, a radical understanding of what it means to successfully negotiate society as Christians, Blacks, and citizens. It is anticipated that, at some point, congregants will fall short of these expectations. Yet they stand as the rubric to which leadership points and membership strives.

As the leadership team is socialized by the pastor, they become the educational team for the entire congregation. The pastor may be expected to spearhead certain teaching/learning events during worship, midweek bible study, and other mass events. However, niche programs, led by vetted clergy and lay staff forward the church's messages in the pastor's stead. For most of the churches in this analysis, the leadership structure is, on the surface hierarchical, but belies a much more collaborative network of church leaders. Yet pastors consider the decision-making processes to be largely democratic and participatory. However, resulting tensions surrounding issues such as succession or when a pastor's vision departs considerably from its previous course can reveal whether congregations are sluggish to change or as adaptive and resilient as large churches are imagined to be. And although the senior pastor plays a pivotal role in the goings on of the church, those who are most discerning appear to be training their replacements as well as preparing the next generation of Black megachurch leaders and members.

Table 3.1 Summary of Black Megachurch Schools

BLACK MEGACHURCH SCHOOLS (N=9)	School Name Establish Date	Grades and No. students	Curriculum	Courses	Afrocentric	Tuition (Per Year)	Uniforms	After/Day care Head Start	Other Features
EMBASSIES OF CHRIST *Gary, IN*	Ambassador Academy Est. 1997 (Accredited)	Daycare-9; 300 students	A Beka: Bible reading/ memorization: Zaner Blosser	Language Arts, Math, Reading, Tech., Gym, Spanish	N	Daycare ($3,400): PreK ($3,250) for K-9; discounts for members	Y	Daycare($): Aftercare($)	Instructional Day Care, 8th grade electives: Home Econ., Dance, Vocal Training
GREATER ALLEN *Jamaica Queens, NY*	The Allen Christian School (ACS) Est. 1982	Pre-K-8	Christian Ed.: Christian Ethics: Spanish Prof. Exam	Music History, Band, Studio Art, Spanish, Technology, Social Studies	N	Pre-K-K ($5,550) for one child: $1^{st} - 8^{th}$ grade ($5,150): Based on enrollment	Y	Extended Day included in tuition for Pre-K and K: programs to transition after ACS	Grades divided into "House Teams": National Jr. Hon. Society
GREATER MT. CALVARY HOLY *Washington, DC*	Calvary Christian Academy Est. 1992 (ICAA)	Pre-K-8: 215 students	A Beka: Positive Action Bible Curriculum: Saxon Math	Math, Reading, Language Arts	N	Pre-K ($4,450): K-8 ($5, 00)	Y	Before and After-care Program ($)	Infant and toddler programs
METROPOLITAN BAPTIST CHURCH *Washington, DC*	The Metropolitan Day School Est. 1998	3yrs-5th grade: 1,000 students: 20:1 student-teacher ratio	Morning Devotions and Bible Study: Core Knowledge Series	Language Arts, Math, Spelling, Science, Social Studies, Geog, History, PE, Arts, Foreign Language	African American Studies	NA	Y	Before and After-care Program ($)	Summer Enrichment Program

Key: ($) means additional fees are required: Ed. = Education: Econ. = Economics: Tech. = Technology: Prof. = Proficiency: Hon. = Honor: Geog. = Geography: PE = Physical Education: Est. = Established: Extracurr. = Extracurricular: no. = number: BA = Bachelor of Arts

Table 3.1 Summary of Black Megachurch Schools (continued)

BLACK MEGACHURCH SCHOOLS (N=9)	School Name Establish Date	Grades and No. students	Curriculum	Courses	Afrocentric	Tuition (Per Year)	Uniforms	After/Day care Head Start	Other Features
NEW BIRTH MBC *Atlanta, GA*	New Birth Christian Academy Est. 1993 (GAC/SACS)	Pre-K–12; 200+ students	SAT, K–11 : OLSAT 2, 4, 6: Kingdom Theology	Music, Math, Performing/Visual Arts, Computer Tech., Foreign Language, PE, Reading, Writing	N	Range= $4,253–$4,961 (varies)	Y	Group, one-on-one, and parent counseling; After care ($)	Academic Summer School (June); Extracurr. Activities; Phonics
SALEM BAPTIST CHURCH *Chicago, IL*	Salem Christian Academy Est. 1990	Pre-K–8; About 500 students	Standardized testing under review (as of 9/8/09); Bible-based	Language Arts, Math, Social Studies, Science, Art, Music, PE, Library, Tech., Dance, Choir	N	$3,650–$11,100 depending on # of children enrolled	Y	Before and After-School Program ($)	After-school program classes; "Excellence in Etiquette" and Karate
ST. STEPHEN *Louisville, KY*	Simmons College of KY (ABHE applicant)	College-age	Certificates: Diplomas: BA: BA in Theology	General Education: Christian college	N	$125 per credit hour	N/A	Counseling	Dr. Kevin Cosby President since 2005
TRINITY UCC *Chicago, IL*	Kwame Nkrumah Academy	K-6	A Beka	Language Arts, Math, Science, Art, Music, PE, Library, African American Studies	Y	Varies	Y	Before and After-School Program: Daycare ($)	African History courses; Library
VICTORY CHURCH *Atlanta, GA*	Victory World Christian School Est. 2006	K–5; About 220 students; 22:1 student-teacher ratio	SAT: A Beka: Rosetta Stone: Professor B	Spanish, Math, Language Arts, Social Studies, Science, Music, Technology, Art, PE, Health	N	$4,830–$4,970	Y	Before and After-Care ($)	Computer lab: Library

Key: ($) means additional fees are required: Ed. = Education: Econ. = Economics: Tech. = Technology: Prof. = Proficiency: Hon. = Honor: Geog. = Geography: PE = Physical Education: Est. = Established: Extracurr. = Extracurricular: no. = number: BA = Bachelor of Arts

Notes

1. Lincoln and Mamiya (1990), Schaller (1990), Thumma and Travis (2007).
2. Niebuhr (1995), Ostling and Hajratwala (1991), Schaller (1990).
3. Refer to Lincoln and Mamiya (1990) about the Black Church priestly/prophetic dialectic. Barnes (2004) shows that priestly church tenets can foster community activism.
4. Harrison (2005).
5. Lincoln and Mamiya (1990), West (1993).
6. Graham (2009), Talbert 2009. Moreover, Garibaldi (1989) predicts that only about half of the HBCUs will survive into the 21st century.
7. Davis (2004), Montecel et al. (2004), Ravitch (2000). For example, in 1996, the reading proficiency for 17-year-old Blacks was equivalent to that of 13-year-old Whites. Similar patterns were evident in science, writing, and math. Increased federal funding for programs such as Head Start and remedial education have resulted in gains in reading and math for children in the most impoverished schools. Yet they continue to lag behind their peers in high SES schools (Hallinan 2001).
8. Charter schools are defined as public schools that have a contract with a local school board or state agency in order to exist. Schools have to maintain specific educational goals, but have much more autonomy than public schools. Religious organizations that can adhere to separation of church and state are able to also apply for charter schools. Blacks are slightly more likely to enroll in charter schools than Whites. However, in locales such as Connecticut, Illinois, and Florida, a disproportionate percentage of Black children attend charter rather than public schools. A 1999 survey found that 60 percent of Blacks support school choice (*Journal of Blacks in Higher Education* 2000–1; Lacireno-Paquet et al. 2002). Scholars such as Davis (2004) contend that technology in response to the digital divide can also be used to compensate for segregated spaces by exposing students to diverse environments, social justice models, and strategies to promote change.
9. Fiske and Ladd (2000), Lacireno-Paquet et al. (2002). The latter authors found that nonmarket-oriented charter schools tend to serve equal or higher proportions of needy populations than public schools. However, more entrepreneurial-oriented charter schools do not. Additionally, Archbald (2004) did not find evidence that magnet schools' availability resulted in class-based segregation among schools.
10. Dee and Fu (2004), Wells et al (2000).
11. Archbald (2004).
12. Ravitch (2000)
13. Archbald (2004), Lacireno-Paquet et al. (2002), Research Policy Practice International (2000), Wells et al. (1998).
14. Studies by Coleman and Hoffer (1987) and Bryk et al. (1993) suggest the Catholic school experience can help offset the Black–White student achievement gap.

15. Ainsworth-Darnell and Downey (1998), Billingsley (1992), Clark (1991), Matthews-Armstead (2002), Nettles (1991).

16. The following 10 churches in this study sponsor GED programs; Allen Temple, Bible Way, Embassies of Christ, Greater Allen, Greater Mt. Calvary, Metropolitan, Ray of Hope, Salem, St. Stephen, and Trinity.

17. Thumma and Travis (2007) challenge this myth as well.

18. Schaller (1990) describes the tendency among megachurches to provide training internally and the potential negative implications such training can have on seminaries and bible colleges should persons seek training from their church rather than at places that have traditionally trained clergy.

19. Anthony (2001), Hill (2007), Seymour (1997), Wimberly (1994).

20. Schaller (1990), Thumma and Travis (2007).

Chapter Four

Empowerment and Liberation Theologies

The Truth Will Make You Free

BY DEFINITION, LIBERATION THEOLOGIES center and celebrate difference. They attempt to turn colonizing influences upend so that marginalized groups become empowered to find intra-group and personal value that has typically been ignored, devalued, or unacknowledged by majority members. However, in order to consider how these paradigms manifest among Black megachurches, it is necessary to examine the influence of an ascriptive characteristic indelibly linked to them—race. I consider how Black megachurch clergy weigh in on issues of race, racism, and Afrocentricity as well as how such sentiments affect the church socialization process. Clergy views on racial matters do not neatly follow abstract models, but are shaped by systemic forces, biblical paradigms, personal experiences, and church context. Some Black megachurch pastors are purposely repositioning how race is framed to create culturally diverse spaces. Others concentrate on the Black experience to illustrate the inherent strength found in "being Black." And still other churches express intangible sentiments about "Blackness" in more pragmatic, tangible ways.

Race Matters and Racial Issues

In *Race Matters*, West (1993) presents a twofold definition of Black authenticity where being Black means experiencing a rich cultural heritage and community *as well as* contending with and combating White supremacy. In *Black Sexual Politics*, Collins (2004) describes a "new racism" that extends prior forms of racial oppression based on a political structure that disenfranchises people of color while feigning a shroud of inclusivity. Even more recently, the same scholar describes the contemporary phenomenon of color-blind racism as a system of power; she provides proactive methods to counter its structural, disciplinary, cultural, and interpersonal domains. Based on the complex nature of such racism, in order to transform society into a more democratic space, Collins (2009) argues for social structures like public education to become steeped in resistance. No matter how it is framed, life in a racially stratified society, segregated spaces, and experiencing racial discrimination continue to take their toll on Blacks and other minorities. Moreover, dynamics such as aversive racism and fair-weather liberals, as well as contemporary rhetoric about colorblindness and a "post-Obama-post-racial" society make identifying the existence and effects of race-related problems and combating them all the more tenuous.[1] Whether Black megachurches ascribe to these views about race and racism, the existence of a primarily Black membership circumscribed in a predominately White society inevitably means that race and related issues surface. The Black Church has a long history of emphasizing Black heritage. According to Lincoln and Mamiya's (1990) national study, almost 65 percent of Black clergy use sermonic references that associate pride, beauty, and power with Blackness. The trend is most evident among younger, better educated pastors, and those affiliated with denominations that attract more economically stable Blacks. Although references to the "Black" experience imply a collective history, the concept has different connotations, even among Blacks. The tendency to acknowledge, understand, and respond to race and racial issues in varied ways is also evident among the Black megachurches studied here.[2]

When describing Black megachurches, Tucker (2002) refers to three continuums linked to worship and architectural styles, Afrocentricity, and church features. Use of a continuum as a descriptive device is not new among research that uncovers heterogeneity in a social setting. In like fashion, I contend that how the sample Black megachurches understand *race and racial issues* is best characterized by a single continuum where more Afrocentric congregations lie on one end of the spectrum and more race-neutral churches lie on the other. Minimally, whether and how *race matters* among Black megachurches influences worship style and iconography. Even churches that can be considered more race-neutral include vestiges of Black Church culture in their musical expressions and sermonic techniques. Some of these holdovers would be difficult to prohibit given a predominately Black membership—many of whom are Black-identified. However, regardless of their congregational position on race issues, all of them sponsor programs and activities specifically geared toward Blacks. Thus even an idealized message that promotes a racially and ethnically diverse congregation does not prohibit programs and services that respond to specific interests, needs, and challenges in the Black community.

Black megachurches described as "unapologetically Black" lie at one end of the continuum. Their position is articulated in mission and vision statements, on church bulletins, and in church logo. Furthermore, a pro-Black focus is evident in sermons as biblical passages and characters are compared and contrasted with the Black experience. Current events indicative of inequities are frequently included. Using Lincoln and Mamiya's (1990) terminology, these churches would be considered *prophetic* because one's salvation experience is expected to accompany commitment to causes associated with social action. These churches not only emphasize Black concerns, but are usually involved in programs to combat social problems in Africa and the plight of other historically oppressed groups in the United States and abroad. Church efforts are designed to instill personal responsibility among Blacks and collective empowerment in the Black community. This understanding is expressed in the following representative quote:

> The Black Church has a responsibility to Black people, but not *exclusively* [emphasis is his] to Black people. Many people say there is no such thing as Black Church, White Church. That's not true. Secondly, [such people incorrect-

ly believe] it's not biblical and it's not theological...if you study the Gospels and
if you study the missionary agenda of evangelists and the mission's movement
in the New Testament, you know that each of the Gospel writers had a particular audience that they were writing to. So Matthew is writing to Jews. Mark
is writing to Romans. Luke is writing to Greeks. John's writing to Hellenists.
Paul was the missionary to the Gentiles. Peter is the missionary to the Jews. So
they had their own homogenous audience that they were attempting to reach.
And the Black Church is not a segregated institution, but it does have a mission to the Black community and beyond. And [name of church] is faithful to
that mission. (pastor of an urban Baptist church in the Midwest)

For the above pastor, his vocation, and that of his congregation are race-
based, influenced by Afrocentricity, and supported by the scriptural
legacy of New Testament writers and early church organizers. This
church embraces a pro-Black stance with a pro-people agenda and does
not consider these perspectives mutually exclusive. However, that was
historically not the case for a Chicago-land congregation affiliated with
the predominately White United Church of Christ:

> When we were started by the denomination in 1961, the desire was, as our
> members put it, 'to have a White church in Black face.' We were *bougie* [empha-
> sis is his and means bourgeoisie]. We were not related to the community. We
> were not related to poor people....We had no gospel music. We had hymns,
> anthems, and spirituals....In 1966 our first pastor left...and the second pastor
> walked in '67, came back here in '68 and 'Negroes' turned 'Black' [referencing
> the change in how Blacks defined themselves as a result of the Black Power and
> Civil Rights Movements]. So we had a Negro church in a Black com-
> munity—and the church started to die. We were over 400 members and
> dropped down to 87. At that point the congregation said, 'We've got to change.
> Are we going to be a church related to the Black community or not?'...so they
> made a conscious decision to be a Black church related to the Black communi-
> ty. We define ourselves, we don't let other people define us.

According to this pastor, the now "unapologetically Black" church
specifically selected him as leader based on the desire to become Black-
focused and responsive to the needs of the predominately Black area in
which they are located. Their need to address Black concerns includes
socializing future generations of Black clergy toward an Afrocentric
posture and subsidizing their education. By formally educating clergy

leaders, the church is, by default, creating spaces where congregants will learn to appreciate diversity in general and Blackness in particular:

> This city has…eleven fully accredited seminaries, but they are White. And a lot of Blacks who get called to ministry here, they get over there…they're turned off by that. So we started pushing at this church…the theology of James Cone, Jackie Grant, and [Katie] Cannon, Douglas, and [Gayraud] Wilmore.

He contends that church leaders responsible for teaching, preaching, and leading must be formally trained in order to properly educate members to have a healthy racial image. The necessity of his viewpoint is corroborated by scholarship that ties racism to economic and emotional trials for Blacks. These Black megachurch pastors appear cognizant of the systemic correlates between race and other quality of life issues outlined in such studies:

> More often than we would prefer, race supersedes economic status (including poverty status) in determining experience, and, profoundly so…race has a deep impact on one's experience. (Johnson 2000: 60)

Furthermore, they are aware of the potentially militating effects Christianity can have against racial inequality and related life stressors:

> The impact of stress can be far reaching and, at times, affect the mental, physical, and sociological state of Black Americans…as it relates to race [and] strain …religiosity can serve as a buffer against the negative effects of emotions. (Gabbidon and Peterson 2006: 91)

In contrast to a strategy of training clergy to be race-conscious, as was done in some Black Church settings in the past,[3] more recently organized Black megachurches or those with younger pastors appear to have a different understanding of race. For them, 9–11 appears to have replaced slavery, the Jim Crow South, and the Civil Rights Movement as a guiding frame of protest. Furthermore, it can be argued that the former catastrophe unified diverse racial groups, if only temporarily, around *Americanness*.[4] It has been suggested that historic Black Church leaders such as Rev. Jesse Jackson have been supplanted by younger, more savvy Black and brown leaders who do not fully appreciate the influence or role of the historic Black Church and its contemporary successor or who actually consider the church archaic and nonresponsive. This means that pastor's age, in part, becomes a proxy for how large Black congregations understand, recollect, and respond to race and episodes such as; the Civil Rights Movement, deindustrialization, 9–11, Jena 6, the Katrina catastrophe, and global capitalism. One experience in the field details how race can be embedded in worship to inform and instruct.

During a Watch Night Service at a Chicago church affiliated with the United Church of Christ,[5] in addition to a bulletin that described the celebration's twofold purpose, attendees were provided with a copy of the Emancipation Proclamation. The influence of race was most evident during the two sermons. References were made to the experiences of Blacks in the Diaspora. A central theme in the first sermon was the tendency by powerful White groups to *sanitize* history as they *canonize* it—and the need for Blacks to proactively write their own histories. Through skillful use of cadence and word mastery, the pastor centered the Black experience in God's purpose for humanity and exegeted a passage from an Afrocentric perspective. The sermon climaxed as he extemporaneously listed the names of U.S. presidents as an example of how secular men of power could not derail God's plan for Blacks. The senior pastor's later sermon focused on an ideology of victory. For him, Blacks, like Israelites, are people of promise living in exile. Both services illustrated the intentional way race and racial issues can be incorporated into worship experiences to not only socialize listeners about their roles and responsibilities as Christians, but as Blacks as well.

Congregations with mission statements or theologies that do not specifically discuss race, ethnicity, or related topics still seem to find themselves addressing these issues. Although one Disciples of Christ church in Atlanta, GA, considers discipleship to be its overarching theme, its clergy representative notes the following: "pastor [name] does preach and teach that [Black Liberation theology], but it is not our primary focus." However, she continues, "she preaches about relationships, racism, and all 'isms' that would separate us." Similarly, the pastor of a Baptist Church in the northeast recognizes its connection to Africa in an important, generalized, but not all-encompassing way:

We are Christian-centric and Afro-*sensitive* [emphasis is his] and those are very intentional words. We actually got that phrase from Dr. Cain Hope Felder when he did our African Heritage lecture series. So no, we would not call it [referring to the church's stance on race] Afro-centric, we would call it Afro-*sensitive*.

And for another midwestern, urban Baptist church, more militant expressions of Black pride have been tempered over time, but have not replaced an Afrocentric posture:

I think that we are Afrocentric. I think that we are necessarily, biologically African. We are unapologetically Christian. And so it is our Christianity that informs everything that we do, but it does not do so to the detriment, to the exclusion, or to the eradication of who we are ethnically and sociologically. We have not retained our posture within the 1960s and we are not raising our fists in protest against the system. But at the same time, we're aware of who we are and we're aware of what we have experienced. What we've come from. What we've come through. We're grateful for all those experiences and determined to live life at another level because of the tremendous sacrifices that have been made by our foreparents…so not to be Afrocentric would be to deny who we are and to deny the validity of what our foreparents did and to bring to shame the millions of persons whose bodies are at the bottom of the Atlantic Ocean through the Middle Passage…so how could we be anything else?

As described by this pastor, history and, for many, daily experiences, make it difficult to separate one's personal racial identity from one's church identity. In this way, contemporary ways of "being Black" for largely formally educated, middle-class congregants are considered authentic expressions of heritage and pride. Thus what it means to be Black can encompass identity as well as outcomes. According to one pastor of a northeastern Baptist church, although his congregation is not Black-centered, it espouses a special message for Black *males* and uses spiritual strategies to model traits that appeal to them. His understanding of gender is infused with race- and liberation-based symbolism:

We are purposed to reach out to men, because Black men are in trouble. We are blessed to have a larger than average Black male population…the strong position of Black Liberation presents a Christianity that is not so effeminate and I *believe* that I am a man and I *think* that I am [emphasis is his]. Men follow a man.

So I do not want to hang it all on me, but I think it is something. I think men follow a man who does not think he is the only man in the building. So I think there are some strategic approaches to brotherhood that I try to establish in my leadership style. My father used to tell me that you can tell a lot about a man's leadership, not by how many people, nor how many women, but how many and what type of men follow him.

The above pastor has been able to attract and maintain a relatively large Black male contingency without alienating his female members by exemplifying a specific Christian image that is both Black and masculine. In addition to associating this stance with their church's identity, the female members appear supportive of this model because they believe that it positively influences their counterparts, helps cultivate more marriageable Black males, and ultimately results in more stable Black families and communities.

Regardless of their perspective on race, most clergy are clear that the programs and events sponsored by their respective churches should respond to concerns in the Black community. However, their ministries do not preclude other racial and ethnic groups—they merely center the Black experience by design. Furthermore, those with long-term goals are also attempting to prepare for future challenges Blacks may face. As noted in scholarship, post-slavery Blacks have a unique experience in the United States that can exact specific tolls:

> Unfortunately, centuries later [i.e., after the Middle Passage], stress remains a part of the Black American experience—so much so, that there is a growing body of literature that examines the dimensions of the stress and the consequences of stress as it relates to being Black…we call this dynamic *living while Black* [emphasis is theirs]…'Black skin exacts a social cost'…there is a special burden of being Black in America. (Gabbidon and Peterson 2006: 84, 100)

A pastor of a relatively new non-denominational church in the Midwest describes an overarching belief that their church's purpose is to address the spiritual and temporal needs of a predominately Black city: "we teach the people here in our ministry—and the things that we do—are really pieces of fulfilling God's purpose for Blacks." Ultimately, empowerment, self-efficacy, and a healthy racial identity are important objectives for such churches—particularly those more directly identified with the Black experience. To them, part of the Black Church's call involves: socializing Blacks to be self-reliant; helping people understand and counter negative societal forces; and, providing the spiritual, intellectual, and practical skills to combat stereotypes, prejudices, and negative outcomes associated with their race and culture.

Race and related themes are most apparent among the sample Black megachurches in iconography, sanctuary displays, bulletins, sermons, and teaching lessons. How race is played out is most evident in programs and ministries associated with combating poverty, prison ministries, job training, health programs, rites of passage events, and youth activities. Some churches reflect Black-*flavor* and others are concertedly Black-identified in posture, purpose, and programming. Yet even the most Black-focused congregations have non-Black members and welcome a diverse populace. It might be argued that those congregations with a substantial White presence are, in their own way, engaged in a resocialization process of their oppressors—an important, but often overlooked dimension of Cone's (1997) formula for systemic liberation. However, this application seems only germane if White members are part of the power elite. My observations suggest that churches that consider themselves unapologetically Black appear to actually be *more* culturally sensitive to issues of diversity and thus strive to create more inclusive spaces. Because such churches are intentional about fostering welcoming and affirming spaces for even the most stigmatized groups in society such as gays and lesbians, persons overcoming substance abuse, and the previously incarcerated, by default, marginalized groups in general are more apt to also feel accepted. And regardless of how inclusivity manifests, each of the churches spearheads programs that address issues germane to Blacks and other historically oppressed groups.

Congregational responses to racial issues are correlated with factors such as location, membership profile, and pastoral beliefs. In addition to their educational background and age, how primary leadership understands race and racial matters shapes how these topics are dealt with in each church. As would be expected, clergy that have been exposed to scholarship regarding the history of race in America, Liberation theologies, and social action tend to lead their congregations in a way that more concertedly infuses issues of religion with race. Older pastors who lived during the Civil Rights Movement and were actively engaged in social justice activities here and abroad also embed race more readily and literally in their church's identities. Additionally, concerns about race from an international perspective are apparent. For example, seven sample churches (43.8 percent) sponsor specific out-reach programs, partner with organizations to provide relief, or have adopted a community or school in Africa. Yet for several pastors who appear less cognizant of major Black theologians and related scholars, location and the desire to improve the life chances in their predominate-ly Black neighborhoods precipitate race-related programs.

Although each clergy described their congregation as either God- or Christ-centered, another appropriate descriptive for most would be *race-informed* (or for several, race-sensitive). This characterization pro-vides a space for various understandings of how churches respond to racial matters. Black megachurches that intentionally have race-neutral logos, worship, and websites,[6] but also sponsor programs geared toward the Black community can be included in this grouping. Even those con-gregations that are unapologetically Black can be included in this cate-gorization because their focus on Black empowerment is not in response to Whites, but rather, because of their intrinsic connection to Blacks. Race-informed also means that, to a large degree (and for several church-es here, continually), central dimensions of church life are specifically framed from a Black perspective. Moreover, resultant programs are about and for Blacks *and other groups* that face similar challenges.

Black megachurches appear positioned to be more proactive rather than reactive to racial concerns. This is not to suggest that smaller Black churches are not attempting to effectively respond to social problems, but rather that because of their resources, structure, and alliances, Black megachurches are often in a better position to do so. Sentiments among these clergy also suggest that some Black megachurches have a stronger, yet non-paternalistic sense of urgency and personal responsibility for the needs of Blacks and groups like them than some of their White megachurch counterparts due largely to their close connection to the people for whom many of the efforts are focused. However, several of the largest churches studied here face a conundrum. How can they effectively present a societal image of color blindness and simultaneously address concerns among a primarily Black congregation located in primarily Black spaces—and without denying the continued systemic, race-related challenges many Blacks face? In contrast, what are the challenges involved in applauding, recognizing, and intentionally teaching and preaching about the strengths found in Black heritage and, when necessary, critiquing the larger society, without being cast as racist? Moreover, can Black megachurches create places of reflection, rest, *and* resistance possible, according to Collins (2009), via visionary pragmatism? These are the types of ideological, sociological, logistical, and practical quagmires through which certain Black megachurches negotiate.

Liberation Theology as a Dimension of Black Megachurch Culture

This project identifies, among other things, ways Black megachurches use cultural tools to *free* adherents from various religious, psychological, emotional, social, and economic *chains* they believe bind them and prevent them from maximizing their potential. According to clergy, living spiritually successful lives represents a minimal requirement for believers. For those who espouse Prosperity theology or related tenets, tangible benefits should also be expected. Although each church approaches the topic differently, they all espouse a message of liberation that is both spiritual and temporal. It is common for pastors to update historic models of liberation for their specific vision, context, and community. Understanding certain theological underpinnings informs broader Black megachurch perspectives and programs.

Theology, the study of how religion is understood, practiced, and experienced, has been the subject of many debates among academicians, bible scholars, clergy, and laypersons. Within Christendom, one's theology is grounded in beliefs about God and God's relationship with humanity. It shapes religious identity and influences seemingly mundane aspects of life.[7] But because beliefs vary and theology is, by definition, an interpretation of religious symbol systems, theologies are numerous and nuanced. King (1994) refers to the variability of Christian theology as "a constructive undertaking" with "no real consensus about either the substance or the task" (pp. 1–2). So although theology is inherently subjective and variable, it is commonly at the heart of a congregation's stance from which other teaching/learning endeavors and programs stem. Moreover, theology is considered a central component of Black Church culture that affects preaching, teaching, and programmatic efforts. Cone (1997) provides a general definition of this biblical interpretive process specifically germane to the Black community:

> The task of theology is to show the significance of the oppressed's struggle against inhuman powers, relating the people's struggles to God's intention to set them free. Theologians must make the gospel clear in a particular social context so that God's people will know that their struggle for freedom is God's struggle too. (Pp. 90–1)

Yet the flexibility of theology becomes apparent as it is informed by factors such as pastoral profile, denomination, and congregant and community concerns. So church theology can be considered a core set of biblically interpreted beliefs from which a broader church stance originates. Although I consider two specific Liberation theologies here, they do not encompass the varied perspectives embraced by the sample Black megachurches that are outside the scope of this study, and range from a Social Gospel message to Prosperity theology. I focus on these two Liberation theologies because they have been largely embraced in religious academic circles and among formally educated Black clergy. Given that Black megachurches have a reputation for readily appropriating many cultural tools, I consider whether liberation perspectives are incorporated as well. Furthermore, I am specifically interested in whether liberation motifs influence educational and instructional spaces. Understanding how Womanist and Black Liberation theologies have been historically understood as well as their use among large Black churches will illumine the potentially enduring effects of longstanding prophetic cultural components. In addition, theological variations will illustrate whether congregation-specific appropriations of the two paradigms educate and empower believers in decidedly different, yet transformative ways.

Black Liberation and Womanist Theologies

Black Liberation theology formally emerged in tandem with the Black consciousness and Civil Rights movements of the 1960s. Yet its presence has been traced back as far as the 16th century and it has direct ties to Latin American Liberation theology. Liberation symbols and themes were apparent both during and after slavery, but were codified by theologians and scholars such as James Cone, Major Jones, De Otis Roberts, Gayraud Wilmore, Jacquelyn Grant, Cornel West, and William Jones. In particular, James Cone's (1969[1999]) *Black Theology and Black Power* is considered by most to be the archetypal analysis of the subject. It describes both the revolutionary as well as routinizing nature of Black religiosity and calls for radical change:

> The task of Black Theology, then, is to analyze the Black man's condition in the light of God's revelation in Jesus Christ with the purpose of creating a new understanding of Black dignity among Black people, and providing the necessary soul in that people, to destroy White racism. (P. 117)

Cone is credited with articulating its premise and primary components as well as delineating this belief system from its counterparts espoused in areas like Latin America. For Cone, the existence of oppression requires use of a radical biblical lens that will transform both the oppressed as well as the oppressor. He posits, "liberation is not an object but the *project* of freedom wherein the oppressed realize that their fight for freedom is a divine right of creation" (Cone 1997: 127). Liberation theology is steeped in education and inherently revolutionary as proponents learn a new way of thinking about themselves that can alter their life trajectories and those of others. Cone (1997) explains its spiritual, existential, temporal, *and educational* dimensions:

> To affirm that liberation is an expression of the image of God is to say not only who God is but also who I am and who my people are. Liberation is *knowledge of self* [emphasis is mine]; it is a vocation to affirm who I am created to be…liberation as the fight for justice in this world has always been an important ingredient in Black religion. (Pp. 134, 141)

Speaking truth to power means Blacks will acknowledge their second-class citizenry just as Whites will own up to their role as facilitators of that same inequality. In doing so, individual and collective self-reflection and the resulting revelations will uncover the futility in oppression and the need for intra- and inter-group reconciliation. Battle (2006) also suggests that, regardless of the theological stance, liberation themes have always been a part of the historic Black Church; "the gift that the Black Church gives to the world is in its beliefs and practice that when any person is mistreated or disadvantaged, an incident of supreme importance has occurred, and something sacred violated" (p. 44). Other scholarship suggests "the Black Church is Black theology in action, and if it keeps a focus on the poor and justice, then it can work for liberation" (Thomas 2004a: xiii). However, given the sexism, homophobia, anti-intellectualism, and, classism evident in certain Black religious circles, some would argue that this theoretically liberating stance has been inconsistently practiced.[8] But contrasting evidence illustrates the singular influence Black churches have played in creating safe havens that foster individual and collective empowerment.[9]

A central tenet of Black Liberation theology is belief in a Black God who is standing in the gap between Black people and all forms of oppression. Just as the bible had been used in the past to justify slavery and Black oppression, this same text of cultural symbols and rituals is now used to challenge Whites, the Black Church, and Black leadership to fight more proactively and concertedly for social justice; "Black theologians began to reread the bible through the eyes of their slave grandparents and started to speak of God's solidarity with the wretched of the earth" (Cone 2004: 10). By raising awareness of the varied manifestations of racism and classism and their deleterious effects, Black Liberation efforts seek to also raise the consciousness of people to counter White supremacy and general societal complacency regarding inequality. A more practical element germane to the current project is its emphasis on Black self-empowerment through education, economic and political advancement, and resourcefulness. This means that in order for Blacks to receive their just do, they have to dramatically alter how they *think about* themselves in relation to groups and organizations that directly or indirectly disenfranchise them. Like Cone, Black Liberationists often contend that the Black community as well as the Black Church have been complacent and complicit in advocating Black power.[10]

The term "Womanist" sprang from a place of exclusion to fuel rallies by Black women on their own behalf and on the behalf of other excluded people. In *Living Stones in the Household of God*, Thomas (2004a) eloquently summarizes the paradigm's essential elements:

> Womanist theology is critical reflection upon Black women's place in the world that God has created and takes seriously Black women's experience as human beings who are made in the image of God....Womanist theology affirms the positive and critiques the negative attributes of the church [refers to the Black Church], the African American community, and the larger society...[it] creates fresh discursive and practical paradigms and "talks back" to structures, White feminists, and Black male liberation theologians. (P. 38)

As transformative models, Black Liberation theology concentrates on race and class issues germane to Blacks in general while Womanist theology focuses on the particular experiences of poor Black women as a rubric to respond to inequities based on gender, race, class, *and* sexual orientation. It is sobering to some persons that Womanist theology largely came about in response to the lack of inclusivity among other oppressed groups. Its emergence is directly correlated with constraints found in two other social movements—the Black consciousness movement spearheaded by Black males and the Feminist movement led by White females. Although both movements positioned themselves as beacons of light against a dark oppressive world, when challenging the status quo, Black males tended to ignore the specific needs of their female counterparts; similarly, White females squeezed out the concerns of their Black counterparts. Battle (2006) provides the following historical observation:

> There were two parallel movements in the USA: Black consciousness and feminist consciousness. Far from working together for social and political reform they viewed each other with suspicion...[yet] Black women were absent from critiques of both racism and sexism. (P. 170)

Yet the tragedy of exclusionary tactics at the hands of other oppressed groups ultimately resulted in a robust, inclusive paradigm that is considered a revolutionary stage beyond both feminist and Black Liberation theologies that, according to Lincoln and Mamiya (1990), represents; a "critique of racism in feminist theology and of sexism in Black theology" (p. 303).

Womanism is also singular because proponents had the audacity to focus their attention on issues and experiences important to Black women.[11] Proponents contend that the model of the poor Black woman provides an understanding of racism, sexism, classism, *and* heterosexism because, as suggested by Cannon (1988), "Black women are the most vulnerable and the most exploited members of the American society" (p. 4). Supporters believe that accepting and inclusive societal spaces will emerge when people who experience oppression as a result of multiplicities of differences become empowered. Other dimensions of this theology include the poor Black woman as a Christ figure; liberation for all oppressed peoples; and validation of the lifestyles, experiences, contributions, and survival strategies of African female ancestors. In a comment particularly germane to this book, Cannon (1988) contends that, although their interests are often ignored, Black women have exhibited an inclusive understanding of thier personhood and purpose:

> The Black female was taught that her education was meant not to "uplift" her alone but also to prepare her for a life of service in the "uplifting" of the Black community...thus teaching became the professional achievement for the Black woman. (P. 48)

Despite its appeal for empathy, universality, and inclusivity, Womanism has not generally been embraced in Black circles—even among more progressive Blacks who support Black Liberation theology. Sexism and hegemony are noted as the primary reasons for this pattern. [12] Like Black Liberation proponents, Womanism as a nontraditional biblical frame of reference, results in a critique of oppressive structures in society as well as practical expectations for redress that require the reconstruction of knowledge in inclusionary ways.[13] The two theologies are also similar because they are typically espoused by an elite set of writers, scholars, and formally educated clerics.

Symbol systems, stories, and other cultural components associated with Liberation theologies emphasize that God recognizes the plight of the oppressed and intervenes both supernaturally and temporally on their behalf. When applied in the Black Church tradition, both perspectives strive to inform oppressed groups about their: singular relationship with God; unique, inherent value both as people and members of society; and, ability to become agents of change. Individual as well as societal transformation will require adherents to proactively challenge secular society and religious organizations, regardless of their racial makeup, if they are found negligent in working for social justice. Furthermore, proponents believe that God is validating their efforts and prophetically working with and through them to alter oppressive spaces. Because both Liberation theologies seem to be best cultivated among Black people and Black churches known for thinking "outside the box," the nontraditionalism associated with the Black megachurch begs the question of whether and how these paradigms are appropriated in these congregations.

Liberation Theologies in Black Megachurch Spaces

By virtue of their audience, pastoral profiles, and connection to the historic Black Church, it is not surprising that many of the Black megachurches here ascribe to Liberation theologies.[14] However, there are inter-church differences as well as differences in how the two theologies are understood and used *within* congregations. Just as Black megachurches are comfortable appropriating a variety of cultural tools in unique ways, many have adapted and altered both theologies to meet their needs. In this section, I juxtapose respective clergy comments about the two Liberation theologies to compare and contrast range of meaning and usage.

For several churches, both perspectives are considered relevant, but are not part of the primary church theological focus. However, they are periodically incorporated by the pastor in teaching/learning activities. Describing the female pastor's Black Liberation usage patterns, one clergy representative from a church in the South notes, "she does make the scripture relevant and not to the exclusion of any group." This same cleric continues by describing how Womanism is displayed:

> She certainly helps us [women] to see ourselves in the Gospels and in the teaching of Jesus Christ, not only that, but our importance in scripture. [Regarding theological focus]...she's not strictly one way or another. We have a large number of female members. Pastor brings that point of view to her teaching and preaching.

Varying degrees of exposure to Liberation theologies are evident. The next church's unapologetically Black perspective means that both liberation perspectives inform the majority of the church's endeavors. However, the pastor acknowledges a particular affinity toward Womanism and its founding proponents:

> I've been in love with it since it first came out. Katy Cannon is a personal friend of mine...Emily Townes. Jackie [i.e., Jacquelyn Grant] came here before she was who she is, before she published, *White Women's Christ, Black Women's Jesus*. Like I try to explain to some of my guys—you don't have to be a female to be a Womanist theologian and Dwight Hopkins is a member here, Linda Thomas is a member here [famous Womanists]. So we affirm it. We embrace it. I think it's much needed because...they're doing such exciting things...[referring to Womanist scholars] 'We hear what you're saying and we're not knocking Black Theology, but you're not including us. And it's time we speak for ourselves and find our own voices and that's very crucial.' It's almost like the African proverb—the little boy asks his father, 'How come the lions are never victorious in these stories? [father replies]...because the lions aren't writing the history. Until the lions write their own history, it will always be the hunter's version of the story.' And sometimes it's intentional, sometimes its sexist, sometimes its ignorance, meaning, I do not even think I can speak for a woman. (pastor of a Church of Christ congregation in Chicago)

The quoted pastor[15] feels comfortable critiquing Black Liberationists' historic tendency to exclude the interests of Black women and other oppressed groups. Although he stands in solidarity with Black women, he also recognizes the inability of Black men to fully understand all of their concerns. Yet his church's contemporary application of both theologies challenges men and women to embrace roles as liberators. His comments also allude to the importance of formal, culturally relative training by clergy where the "word of Black theology becoming flesh [means] doing Black theology" (Wright 2004: 22–23) through community action. A midwestern Baptist pastor describes vestiges of self-hatred among Blacks as a result of negative systemic forces—and the importance of Black Liberation theology to facilitate socio-emotional and psychological *freedom*:

> I think one of the sins of Blacks, is what Na'im Akbar calls 'alien self-deformity' or 'anti-self deformity' and that is—Black people do not like themselves. Alien self-deformity manifests itself in 'good hair'—but what constitutes good hair? Good hair is hair that covers your head. But because of our orientation, we think good hair is hair that approximates White folk's hair. That's alien self-deformity, which is a sin. So Black Liberation theology broadens what sin is. It's more than just sexual immorality but, it's also about not loving yourself because you think something is wrong with you because you have a wide nose or big lips or Black women got big behinds. God made Black people and God was not guilty of any form of creative malfeasance and so the images around [church name]—you see a lot of positive Black images, yet not exclusively Black images. And that is in order to combat the pathology of alien self-deformity or anti-self deformity.

The above pastor recognizes and embraces Cone's (1969[1999]) original intentions for liberation. He also suggests that today's version of Black Liberation theology expands the concept of sin and speaks to even seemingly mundane aspects of human existence (for example, how Blacks views their hair) because these issues inform a broader understanding of self-acceptance and God's purposed creation of humanity—including people of color. Without being dogmatic or judgmental, his stance required a proactive response to denominational sexism regardless of the repercussions:

> Our church was the first Black Baptist church in the state of Kentucky to license and ordain women. We have women preachers and our state convention for the most part does not embrace that. In fact, I'm the president of [college's name], but at one time, I was alienated from [college's name], back in the early 80s, because of my Womanist leanings. I've come full circle. [However] I don't try to impose my Womanist views on other churches or other people.

Although certain pastors are more vocal about their liberationist views, the following pastor of a Baptist congregation in Ohio illustrates how time can alter the intensity, but not the nature, of his use of Black Liberation theology:

> I'm familiar with it [Black Liberation theology], studied with persons who were the proponents of it, incorporate it into my own teaching and preaching. I'm not sure the congregation has much of a self-conscious sense of it, except that when they hear me talking about those themes—God's interest in the poor and the marginalized—they would affirm them....I think it's informative ...So what James Cone and others were doing at that time was to stretch the claims of the Gospel to include issues that heretofore had gone unaddressed by the major shapers of Western theology....It was a necessary additive to what was going on at the time.

When queried regarding Womanist theology, he notes:

> We have multiple women on staff and have had women come to play multiple roles in our church. We have female deacons—which most Baptist churches do not. Yes, so we are trying to help others who don't see that that too is part of the claim of the scriptures. Women can have any role in the church that a man can have. [jokingly] They just can't have *my job right now—not right now* [emphasis is his]. Now maybe when I'm gone they can have it, but short of that, anything else. We have women who have been Chairman of the Trustee Board and of course we have female clergy, ordained, and still in training.

For him, Liberation theologies influence the substance of his teaching and preaching efforts and are also reflected in church programs to address poverty and gender inclusivity. Yet another leader's Washington, D.C., neighborhood precipitates embracing Liberation theologies:

> As a consequence [of the church location], there has never been a moment when this church could fail not to be a part of Liberationist theology, because we dealt with people who seek liberation and we deal with structures that militate against liberation. And so it is our opinion that the Gospel itself is a liberating instruction and therefore in order to be an authentic representative of the living Christ, we can't do anything but espouse Liberation theology.

Like another previously cited cleric, the above pastor describes instances of being ostracized because of his church's position about nontraditional gender roles. Yet he considers the Gospel message the impetus for his church's position:

I think it's a necessary theology [Womanist theology]....We espouse it....Women have a full place at [church name], whether it is at the door as an usher or in the pulpit as a preacher. There is no arena in the life of this church in which women are excluded. We've gone through some things to see that that was the case. About 20–25 years ago, I ordained the first woman in this church to the Gospel ministry. As a consequence, I was put out of the minister's conference because I took that position that we are all equal in the presence and in the sight of God.

However, the following two leaders embrace Black Liberation theology, but only espouse *aspects* of a Womanist perspective they believe do not undermine Black male empowerment:

I am familiar with Womanist theology. And yes, where we differ as it relates to the traditional Baptist church is we do affirm woman in ministry...we affirm the humanity of woman and ability for them to operate in leadership without necessarily abandoning some of traditional position as it relates to male headship. (pastor of Baptist church in the Northeast)

When I think of Womanist theology, the first thing that comes to mind is the Mother-God concept...just the inclusion of females in some ways that I think is designed for men. So it's a little unsettling for me sometimes because it seems sometimes that my sisters, my daughters, my mothers are pressing a point that may not need to be pressed if we understand that we're all equal in God....Because we're talking about the Spirit...then we can still embrace terms like 'Our Father' and be ok...I want equality for women...and I understand the biblical traditions that had women subjugated...but in many ways, I like to think that we've past that in our own culture and I'd like to think that, if God can use a man like me, then He can also use a women like you. (pastor of a non-denominational church in the South)

The above two quoted clergy cautiously espouse Womanist dimensions that do not supplant certain historic male privileges in family and church settings. Also questioned is the imperative to use inclusive biblical language not ascribed in the King James Bible. They affirm women and support female church leadership, but appear to have certain spheres in which men and women are equal and others in which their roles are complementary. Their comments corroborate what theologians such as

Cannon (1998), Cone (2004), Mosby-Avery (2004), and Thomas (2004) consider the most pressing challenge for Black Liberationists—advocating full gender inclusivity.

Yet both paradigms are readily embraced at a West coast Baptist congregation and continually used and practiced by the pastor and other clergy leaders:

> [pastor's name] is really the person who started that type of theological preaching here....And it is certainly based in his training. He believes, like Dr. James Cone believes, people of color have been marginalized and you have to show them that God cares for them as well.

In addition, emphasis on Womanism is apparent in clergy training and visible leadership roles:

> [pastor's name] ordained [name of female clergy], when other people would not. You will find the majority of our ministries are headed by women preachers. Womanist theology allows us to look through the lens to how we see scriptures; we understand that there continues to be discrimination based on your gender, class....Women's theology is taught to our ministers in training....It is embraced in response to their ordination papers; they have to demonstrate full understanding of Womanist theology.

According to this aforementioned clergy, ordination at her congregation is impossible unless ministerial candidates espouse Black and Womanist perspectives, acknowledge that marginalization of these groups continues today, and commit to fight inequality. Moreover, leadership must be able to analyze scripture critically to avoid applying it in oppressive ways. Several congregations have men and women co-pastors. However, as illustrated here, the senior pastor is male:

> Yes. I studied it while working on my Master of Divinity degree. I do embrace that theology [Black Liberation]....I'm familiar with Womanist theology in the sense that I believe women have the same right to ministry as men do. In terms of co-pastor [wife's name], we share equal footing in the church, but I'm the senior pastor. But she has just as much authority as I do, but somebody has to be the designated head—and I am. (pastor of Holiness church in the Washington, D.C., area)

The pastor believes his shared pastoral position is equitable, and he contends that he serves as the senior pastor largely for practical reasons.

Just as he accepts the role, his wife consents to this leadership structure as well.

With the exception of one Baptist congregation, clergy suggest that women can hold any position at their respective churches. By and large, more churches espouse both Black Liberation and Womanist theologies than not. However, the former perspective appears to be more intricately enmeshed in church stances as well as in sermonic and teaching activities and the latter, a more practical and logical application of church roles. Support of Black Liberation theology translates into intentional, strategic emphasis on issues germane to the Black community as well as programs to empower it and other vulnerable groups. However, when queried about Womanist issues, most clergy are more likely to illustrate the *ways* this theology is evident in their congregation rather than whether and how the church's specific theological perspective is influenced by Womanism. The common sense approach in which women are included juxtaposed with the more spiritual mandate relative to racial issues implies that racial issues may take precedence over gender concerns in many of these congregations. If this is the case, "cause competition" may ultimately mean that certain issues germane to women are ignored, despite the fact that;[16] "questions of race and racism are two avenues womanists use to articulate the concerns of Black women...and the dismantling of evil" (Townes 2006: 58).

Another subtle instance of limited embeddedness of the spirit of Womanism is the largely absent use of gender-neutral biblical language. Few churches use the New Revised Standard version of the bible and God continues to be "He." The descriptives for God of Father *and* Mother were incorporated in the pastor's discourses at only one of the churches in this study. Yet the practical application of Womanist theology among the majority of these congregations contrasts with existing studies regarding gender exclusion among Black churches in general.[17] For example, although over 65 percent of Black Church congregants are women, men continue to hold the majority of leadership roles.[18] However, the vast majority of Black megachurches here promote women's presence, affirmation, and acceptance in each echelon of the church. This translates into spaces where Black women can be empowered symbolically and literally in ways that are prohibited in many other societal spaces. Because Liberation theologies ultimately promote freedom from various forms of oppression, markers of their success in Black megachurch spaces reflect, in part, how Black heritage is espoused and expressed as well as how women can participate as leaders or minimally witness others like themselves in key leadership roles. Yet because Womanism does not appear to be embedded in the theological postures of many of these churches, it is unclear whether they are concertedly engaged in efforts to combat inequality in its many forms.

Modeling the Impact of Liberation Theologies on Educational Programs

Clergy interviews illustrate how Liberation theologies are understood and appropriated among the 16 profiled Black megachurches. Findings in this section provide a complementary quantitative examination of the same subject for Black churches of varying sizes, including Black megachurches. Regression modeling is used to test whether Liberation theologies influence Black Church sponsorship of educational programs such as tutoring/literacy, voter education, employment education, and computer training as well as religious educational programs beyond Sunday school. I make use of the same national sample of Black churches referenced in earlier chapters to determine the potential influence of church size and other pastoral and congregational features on educational program sponsorship.

I am specifically interested in the effects of sermons that focus on Black Liberation and Womanist theologies. Although it would be ideal to test the theologies separately, the variable in these secondary data reflects both types of Liberation theologies combined. The same indicators used in the previous chapter are tested here (i.e., church size, Baptist denomination, urban locale, pastor's education and paid status, practical and spiritual sermons, whether churches espouse a social justice focus, and whether they attempt to assimilate new members quickly). A total of 10 independent variables are examined in each of the five models. Although these variables do not represent all possible dynamics that affect whether educational programs are offered, they have been associated with Black Church programs in other studies and thus may be germane here. Table 4.1 summarizes the modeling results. Highlights are provided here and the actual regression output is provided in the appendix.

As evident in Model 1 (and as expected), larger Black churches are more likely to sponsor tutoring or literacy programs for children and teens than smaller ones. Although Baptist churches are generally less apt to provide tutoring/literacy programs than their non-Baptist counterparts, churches with more formally educated pastors are more likely to provide them than those with less formally educated pastors. Neither urban locale nor pastor's paid status play a crucial role in explaining program sponsorship as defined here. However, I am most curious about the influence of Liberation theologies. These findings show that Black churches that are more frequently exposed to sermons about Black Liberation and/or Womanist theologies are actually 1.2 times more likely to sponsor tutoring/literacy programs for youth than churches with less or no sermonic exposure to these two theologies. In the next model about voter education and registration programs (Model 2), four variables are focal. Frequent exposure to Liberation theologies during sermons continues to be important and increases chances that Black churches will provide these types of voter education programs by a factor of 1.4. Denominational differences are not apparent, but church size continues to matter and so does pastor's education. Lastly, as one might anticipate, churches that tend to have a social justice focus are 1.4 times more likely to sponsor voter education/registration programs than churches with less or no social justice emphasis.

Model 3 considers whether Black churches provide employment counseling, placement, or training programs. The previous pattern continues. Those Black churches that more frequently expose congregants to Liberation theologies via sermons are also 1.2 times more likely to sponsor employment educational programs. Moreover, larger Black churches are more apt to sponsor these job-related programs. Furthermore, social justice–focused churches, those that provide practical sermons more frequently, and those that strive to assimilate new members efficiently are also more likely to sponsor these employment-related programs. In light of the digital divide in the Black community,[19] the fourth test considers whether churches offer computer training programs (Model 4). Four variables help predict these efforts; frequent exposure to Liberation theologies, church size, pastor's education, and new member socialization efforts. More frequent exposure to Womanist and Black Liberation sermons are directly related to sponsorship of computer training programs by a factor of 1.2.

The above modeling results illustrate that Black churches continue to offer practical educational programs and some of the church features that make sponsorship more likely. But can the same be said for religious programs? Groundbreaking scholarship by Dubois (1903[2003]), Mays and Nichols (1933), Frazier (1964), and Lincoln and Mamiya (1990) describe common religious programs in the Black Church tradition such as Sunday school and bible study. The final model examines the types of programs that move beyond expected Christian Education programs to provide more in-depth exposure to religious subjects. The dependent variable includes the following seven groups of programs: bible study other than Sunday school; theological or doctrinal study; prayer and meditation groups; spiritual retreats; parenting or marriage enrichment; youth programs; and, programs for young adults and singles. Four predictors emerge (Model 5). First, more frequent exposure to Liberation theologies is correlated with increased sponsorship of these types of religious programs. Additionally, as Sunday church attendance increases so do efforts to provide diverse religious programs. Finally, Black churches that emphasize social justice as well as those that attempt to assimilate new members efficiently sponsor more of these types of religious educational programs.

What do these empirical results mean—especially to readers less interested in statistical tests? First, a consistent pattern across the five models illustrates that church size does matter. This shows that as the number of Sunday worshippers increases, so does the likelihood that Black congregations will sponsor educational programs that are practical and religious in nature. Furthermore, Liberation theologies matter; more frequent sermonic emphasis on subjects associated with freedom from marginalization for Blacks and women tends to be linked to varied religious and non-religious educational efforts. Although the effects of church size may not be a big surprise to readers, this result is important because it quantifies its influence. It also clearly informs us about the connection between "megachurch" size and the types of programs they potentially sponsor. However, the positive influence of Liberation theology sermons may be surprising to some readers. Yet it reminds us of the effects intangible Black Church cultural components can have on tangible outcomes. Lastly, the positive influence of the senior pastor's education works in conjunction with the other indicators to foster these educational efforts.[20]

A few comments are in order about some of the other tested variables that are not significant as defined here. It would be imprudent to suggest that "urban location" does not influence whether churches offer employment programs—previous studies show the contrary.[21] The modeling results uncover the most important indicators from the group of variables that were examined in this particular data. This means that, relative to the 10 variables that are considered, only a select number are directly telling. The goal here was to test a subset of features found to be important in other, largely qualitative, research on Black religiosity in order to focus on two primary characteristics—church size and exposure to Liberation theologies. Without over-stepping the predictive bounds of these results,[22] the consistent, positive influence of Liberation theologies on educational efforts alludes to a broader understanding of what it potentially means to be "liberated." A radical religious and spiritual fervor lie at the heart of Liberation theologies. Yet a temporal requirement cannot be ignored. Both theologies suggest that with the advent of religious freedoms, a host of other liberties should come. People cannot genuinely enjoy some without the others. And churches that espouse liberation tenets are compelled to connect their religious message to *real-world* programs that meet *real* needs—both practical and spiritual.

Conclusion: Liberation Theologies in the New Millennium

The qualitative and quantitative results in this chapter suggest that exposure to Liberation theologies helps foster education-related programs among Black churches in general; church size is also directly influential. Additionally, Black megachurches that espouse Black Liberation theology have been able translate its message—historically confined to largely elite academic circles—to the masses. Moreover, churches that embrace Womanism position themselves to take advantage of the range of gifts and talents female members have to offer. They also positively expand the knowledge and experiential base for male and female congregants. Both these liberative messages seem to have taken on fresh perspectives in church spaces that are non-conformist by design. Their influence across the study churches suggests that these paradigms may be beginning to pass the hurdles of accessibility and practical church relevance that concerned their academic proponents.[23] For a quarter of the Black megachurches here, Womanism is an integral part of church identity. Yet the degree to which Womanism is an intricate part of the other churches that purport it more practically still remains unclear. If its inclusion is largely pragmatic and devoid of introspection, Black megachurches have missed an opportunity to create genuinely inclusive spaces. Most importantly, they are less likely to fully acknowledge the continued "tridimensional phenomenon of race/class/gender oppression" Black women still face (Cannon 2004: 68).

Black megachurch "feminist pastors" have been accused of largely providing lip service to the concerns of Black women[24] while negative images of Black females such as the "mammy, the emasculating bitch, the tragic mulatta, the castrating matriarch, and the pickaninny continue to ooze from the pores of videos and magazine and television and radio and music and the pulpit" (Townes 2006: 3). So although the inclusivity evident among a substantial number of Black megachurches here is noteworthy, their efforts would invariably be critiqued by Liberation theologians who would challenge them to more concertedly and visibly *write Black women and other oppressed groups* into their respective church histories, legacies, and overall church stances. Even among the most intentional Black megachurches here, continued instructional steps are warranted in order to create "a God-talk and God-walk that are holistic, seeking to address the survival and liberation issues of women, men, children, workers, and gays and lesbians" (Cannon 1988: 42).[25] Most of the Black megachurches here appear to be on their way, but I wager that most would agree that they still have a ways to go before they can honestly claim completely liberated church spaces.

Table 4.1: Regression Modeling Results for Black Church Education Programs

Modeling Question: Churches that have this feature (listed vertically in the left-most column) also tend to be more likely to sponsor these educational programs than churches that do not have this feature? (Y="Yes" and Odds for Models 1-4 are provided in parentheses)

	Types of Educational Programs				
	Model 1 Tutoring	Model 2 Voting	Model 3 Employment	Model 4 Computer	Model 5 Religious
Liberation Theologies					
Black Liberation/Womanism	Y (1.2)	Y (1.4)	Y (1.2)	Y (1.2)	Y
Church Size					
Church Attendance	Y (1.0)	Y (1.0)	Y (1.0)	Y (1.0)	Y
Other Church Demographics					
Urban location (1=yes)	N	N	N	N	N
Baptists (1=yes)	Y (0.8)	N	N	N	N
Pastor's Profile					
Pastor's Education	Y (1.2)	Y (1.4)	N	Y (1.2)	N
Paid Pastor	N	N	N	N	N
Church Dynamics					
Sermons: Practical Advice	N	N	Y (1.3)	N	N
Sermons: Spirituality	N	N	N	N	N
Social Justice Environment	N	Y (1.4)	Y (1.4)	N	Y
Assimilates New Members	N	N	Y (1.2)	Y (1.2)	Y

Interpret each model vertically. Models 1–4 are logistic regression models and Model 5 is a negative binomial model. Odds are only appropriate for Models 1–4. All predictive variables are statistically significant at $p<.05$ or greater. Faith Factor 2000 data. Tutorial programs include literacy programs. Voting programs include voter education and voter registration programs. Values less than 1 in parentheses represent a negative relationship between the two variables. $N=1,863$. Actual model output provided in the appendix.

Notes

1. A few studies on the subject include: Billingsley (1992); Bonilla-Silva (2006); Brown et al. (1999); Collins (2000); Feagin (2006); and, Gallagher (2008). Collins (2004) posits that "new racism" is a result of global capitalism that disadvantages people of African descent. It is dependent on mass media for support and reproduction. She argues that new racism is particularly troubling for Blacks and manifests tangibly in education, healthcare, housing, and employment.

2. Thumma and Travis (2007) reference several small studies on megachurches where racial diversity is accomplished by appealing to a broad audience using secular strategies and niche groups. However, studies on racial/ethnic dynamics suggest that the issue is not simply whether diversity exists, but which groups shape church foci and programs, the racial/ethnic profile of persons in power, whether issues germane to diverse groups are addressed or whether a "color-blind" approach is espoused that, despite good intentions, ultimately centers the White experience at the expense of minorities (Allport 1966; Blumer 1958; Collins 2000; Cone 1969[1999], 1995; Feagin 2006; Gallagher 2008; Lincoln 1984; Omi and Winant 1994).

3. Historically, Black Church clergy, especially pastors, were also community leaders. The church was also the grooming ground for Black community leaders (Lincoln and Mamiya 1990).

4. Refer to West's (1993) presentation of the common humanness and Americanness that persons must acknowledge to overcome racism.

5. This service occurred on December 31, 2007 (10:00 p.m. to 12:45 a.m.) at one of the sample churches. Watch Night Service is a worship event to commemorate the end of one year and to "watch" in a new one. In some Black religious circles, it also commemorates the Emancipation Proclamation and the end of chattel slavery that occurred 1 second after midnight January1, 1863. A complementary service was also held from 7:00–9:00 p.m. for persons unable to attend the later service. I attended both. Worship included activities such as praise team-led singing, call-and-response, adult and young dancers, hymns, and a communal scripture.

6. My participant observation experiences at the two churches suggest use of a race-neutral stance largely as a marketing strategy to broaden audience appeal and potentially grow the congregational base rather than attempts to disassociate themselves from the Black experience. The two congregations represent two of the largest "Black" megachurches in the country, but are closely networked with the White evangelical community. They desire to be known as "God's" church, rather than a "Black" church. This positioning is also better informed by race literature on dominant/subordinate relations that shows the tendency to use descriptives that identity and classify minorities, but less so for Whites.

7. Cone (1969[1999]), Hodgson and King (1994), King (1994).

8. For a few considerations, see Barnes (2006) about sexism, Collins (2000) and

Dyson (1996) about sexism and homophobia, and West (1993) about Black sexuality in general.

9. Billingsley (1992, 1999), Lincoln and Mamiya (1990), Wilmore (1994, 1995).

10. Ibid. Also refer to Cone (1969[1999], 1995, 2004), Mosby-Avery (2004), West (1999) and Wilmore (1994, 1995). Research shows the influence and usage of Black Liberation theology by Black churches has varied from two-thirds in some studies to under 35 percent in others. Its use varies based on factors such as denomination and pastor's age and education, as well as overall church class composition. Denominations comprised of more poor persons and less formally educated clergy tend to be less cognizant of Black Liberation theology. For example, AME churches are influenced by Black Liberation theology significantly more than their COGIC counterparts (Calhoun-Brown 1999; Lincoln and Mamiya 1990).

11. Grant's (1989) *White Women's Christ and Black Women's Jesus: Feminist Christology and Womanist Response* stands as the touchstone analysis of Womanist theology; also refer to Thomas (1998). Cannon (2004) describes Womanism as inherently inclusive and interested in causes that impact the Black family, African women and other women of color worldwide, as well as processes, including academic endeavors, that construct knowledge in oppressive ways and ignore Black female presence and contributions. She posits that unlike White feminist theology, Womanism does not create an oppositional space between males and females. In terms of a revisionist account of history, Townes (2006) clearly suggests, "we cannot remember what we never knew" (p. 91). Lastly, Floyd-Thomas (2006) provides a variety of methodologies that will enable researchers to write "Black women back into history" (p. 106).

12. Although Lincoln and Mamiya (1990) support this premise, they also note the potential progressive nature of certain churches that seem priestlier in stance.

13. Lincoln and Mamiya (1990), Mitchem (2002), Thomas (1998). Thomas (2004a) explicates how a Womanist stance can be used to reconstruct knowledge by purposely including once silenced voices and advancing a "new epistemology of holistic survival and liberation" (p. 42).

14. Wright (2004) explains that whether and how Black theology is used in Black churches is shaped by church location as well as the perspective of the pastor and congregants. He emphasizes the type of formal training pastors and clergy receive. Clergy who have only been exposed to seminary training in predominately White spaces or to Eurocentric theological models will be less likely to be exposed to or espouse Liberation theologies.

15. He refers to Townes' (2006) *Womanist Ethnics and the Cultural Production of Evil*, Cannon's (1988) *Black Womanist Ethics*, and Thomas' (2004a) *Living Stones in the Household of God*.

16. Barnes (2006).

17. Giddings (1984), Gilkes (2001), Grant (1989), Higginbotham (1993), Lincoln and Mamiya (1990).

18. In *Black Sexual Politics*, Collins (2004) describes the context needed to cultivate gender inclusivity; "Black women can never become fully empowered in a context that harms Black men, and Black men can never become fully empowered in a society in which Black women cannot fully flourish as human beings" (p. 7).

19. Mossberger et al. (2003), Norris (2001).

20. Barnes (2004, 2005), Lincoln and Mamiya (1990).

21. Billingsley (1992, 1999), Lincoln and Mamiya (1990).

22. Data constraints are outlined in the appendix.

23. Battle (2006), Cannon (1988), Cone (1969[1999], 1995, 2004), Thomas (2004), Townes (2006).

24. Refer to Lee's (2005) detailed analysis and critique of the feminist position of pastor T.D. Jakes.

25. It is not an oversight that sexual orientation and inclusivity are not examined in this book. These subjects are focused on in considerable detail in another future work on Black megachurches by this author.

Chapter Five

Programs to Rightly Divide

Black Megachurch Profiles

CONVENTIONAL EFFORTS TO PROVIDE EDUCATIONAL OPPORTUNITIES are apparent among the Black megachurches profiled here—50 percent of them sponsor Day Schools or academies. More often than not, churches also spearhead innovative methods that expand both the understanding of what it means to *instruct* and how such processes should take place. This chapter deviates from earlier ones because of its largely applied and descriptive nature. Prior chapters focus on how Black megachurches use cultural tools to educate and empower. Here I provide specific descriptions of programs to meet those objectives—what congregations are doing to effect educational change. The chapter has a threefold purpose—first, to detail diverse programs, ministries, and best practices, particularly those that represent nontraditional strategies; second, to examine context-specific efforts; and third, to offer a broad blueprint for spearheading similar activities. Profiles of the 16 sample Black megachurches include brief church histories, "highlights" of distinctive church features, and clergy comments.[1] The chapter ends with a typology of the respective church programs and implications for Black megachurch educational efforts. Several acknowledgments must be made. Space does not permit detailed or exhaustive information. Moreover, profiles do not do justice to the church programs in terms of purpose, complexity, and scope. Yet the goal is met to broadly illustrate the primary efforts these Black megachurches have made to facilitate personal and collective empowerment through education.

Allen Temple Baptist Church—Oakland, California (senior pastor: Dr. J. Alfred Smith, Jr. and pastor emeritus: Dr. J. Alfred Smith, Sr.)

Organized in 1919 as a Northern Baptist mission, Allen Temple has grown from 21 members to over 5,500 members and in excess of 50 active ministries. The church sponsors extensive international and national HIV/AIDS programs and has been engaged in prison ministry for over 30 years. The latter program includes GED preparation, training, and job placement for violent and non-violent ex-offenders. Five 501c3 corporations are housed under the church's non-profit umbrella. The pastor emeritus' following remarks summarize the church's spiritual and secular educational thrusts:

> The Black child is at risk. The Black child is becoming a vanishing species. And it seems the state has only one 'solution' for the 'salvation' of the Black child: more detention centers, jails, and prisons. They who control the shaping of budgets would rather spend $30,000 a year to house a Black prisoner than $15,000 a year to send a Black intellectual youth to Stanford University. (Smith and Kilgore 2006: 36)

Educational Highlights

Allen Temple's prison program includes mock interviews, presentation skills, money management, role-playing, and career planning. Training programs focus on: pre-apprenticeship and construction; culinary arts; cosmetology and barbering; landscaping and horticulture; security; custodial work; technology; and, GED acquisition. Participants also learn to create résumés, search for employment, develop a positive work ethic, and locate private funds to pursue higher education. Referrals are made via case managers, parole officers, and church marketing. According to Pastor Smith; "ninety-five percent of our graduates do not return to prison" (Smith and Kilgore 2006: 17). The church also sponsors anger management classes for Black males who must attend in lieu of incarceration. Other instructional programs and/or ministries include summer algebra and music academies, a Hispanic Ministry, scouting, tutorials, Head Start, couples counseling, parenting classes, and a fully accredited Leadership Institute that provides a two-year course of study to earn a certificate in Christian Ministry.

Antioch Baptist Church—Cleveland, Ohio (senior pastor: Dr. Marvin A. McMickle)

Organized in 1893 by 29 persons, Antioch has over 2,800 members. Based on its architecture, it was designated an historical landmark in 1975. The church is also historically unique in its appointments of formally educated and trained pastors as well as its emphasis on education and political activism as a means of mobility and racial uplift. Pastor McMickle is politically involved and served as a super-delegate during the 2008 U.S. Presidential elections. The church tithes 10 percent of its annual income back into the community. The Genesis Program was created in 2001 as a faith-based career developing ministry to provide training and employment services for the poor. Community programs are sponsored under the Antioch Development Corporation, a 501c3 CDC.

Educational Highlights

In 1999, Antioch became the first U.S. church to open an HIV/AIDS testing center, AGAPE. In partnership with Cleveland Clinic, it provides free, faith-based access to testing, prevention education, case management, referrals, and spiritual as well as risk reduction counseling to over 1,000 people annually. According to the pastor:

It began as a testing center here in April of that year, then expanded into local hospitals....We're in all of the local Planned Parenthoods and now we're in almost all of the Cleveland high schools...and we're moving out into outer ring suburbs as well in partnership with the administrations in those schools....In fact, what tends to happen in our case is that other pastors just send folks to us.

AGAPE is an exclusive HIV education and testing agent for every Planned Parenthood of Greater Cleveland site. It is also an exclusive syphilis prevention education provider for adolescents affiliated with the Cleveland School District and Job Corp. Since 1999, AGAPE has provided services to over 6,000 persons. In 2004, the church introduced, SAMM (Stopping AIDS is My Mission), which trains at-risk Black, Latino, and White students ages 13–18 years old in the Cleveland Municipal Schools to become peer educators.[2] They work with professionals from the SAMM and AGAPE programs to conduct educational seminars with other teens.[3] SAMM has provided HIV prevention education to over 2,000 11th graders in every Cleveland municipal high school. Similar efforts targeting sixth grade boys occur during the Molding Minority Youth Thru Faith and Mentoring (MMYFAM) Program.

Bible Way Church of Atlas Road—Columbia, South Carolina (senior pastor: Elder Darryl Jackson)

Dedicated in 1963 and located on a 125-acre campus, Bible Way is a non-denominational Pentecostal church with over 60 ministries. Its pastor, Elder Darryl Jackson, is a state senator. The church is one of the largest Black employers in the area with about 125 personnel on its over $3 million payroll. In addition to its free meals programs that fed over 40,000 persons in 2007, a planned community is under way via the church's CDC that includes office space, commercial space, a healthcare facility, as well as educational, recreational, housing, and civic facilities. In regard to his congregation's extensive community renewal projects, the pastor notes: "it's very important for believers and places of faith…to make a difference in society, and we think this is our contribution…to really try to improve the community."[4]

Educational Highlights

To encourage home ownership, in 2007, the church sponsored a Homebuyers Education Series and Bank Day event. In response to healthcare needs, the church funds back-to-school physicals for youth, flu shots for the elderly, and free health screenings. In 2007, the church reached over 1,000 youth via various drug prevention activities. A series of violent youth deaths prompted the pastor to institute the Be Right! Project designed to mentor and proactively engage at-risk youth. The program attempts to counter bullying, peer pressure, and gang-related problems by providing interventions, advocacy, and counseling. The church's Emerging Generation Leadership Institute also offers an oppor-tunity for young adults aged 18–35 years to develop leadership skills, tour government agencies, and study business models that foster entre-preneurial expertise. According to the pastor, the program gives partic-ipants "the opportunity to see how the world operates politically and in business."[5]

Embassies of Christ—Gary, Indiana (co-pastors: Revs. Cedric and Joyce Oliver)

Embassies of Christ (EOC) was founded in October 1990 by 12 members and now has over 70 ministries. Both pastors are products of the local community and became full-time ministers after long secular careers. They believe that their calling is to specifically bring God's "kingdom" to earth in an economically challenged urban space. The new $8 million sanctuary that opened in 2007, the Diplomat Center, is a three-block cam-pus that houses a 7,200 square foot gymnasium and a full-sized kitchen. Day care, theatrical productions, and conferences are held at the main campus; other church programs take place at the second campus. According to Pastor Cedric Oliver, strategically-developed church pro-grams attempt to bridge the gap between the spiritual realm and chal-lenges associated with poverty:

> As an inner-city pastor, I've rejoiced watching many sinners walk the aisles and approach the altar in tears to repent. Unfortunately, many people struggling with various issues share similar persuasions. They often think, 'after I give my life to Jesus, my troubles will be over.' Nothing could be farther from the truth. There are indeed substantial supernatural benefits of having a relationship with Christ…when we practice the principles of God, we reap the benefits of His promises. (2005: 19, 72)

Through its CDC, the church also created the Transitional Housing Program for poor families that pays both rent and utilities for three families for no more than two years to enable them to become more economically stable and acquire their own residence. Participants are required to attend church regularly, receive financial counseling, have consistent employment, and financially contribute to a local church.

Educational Highlights

The church's 300-student school, Ambassador Academy, provides instruction for students kindergarten to 9th grade. High unemployment and related poverty and crime in their city precipitated a series of employment initiatives, particularly for Black males. Through its job training program, Diplomat Car Care Center, the church hires unemployed and underemployed people as car detailers and helps prepare them for the general job market. In addition to employment, the program's broader goal is to train full-time and targeted part-time employees in job readiness and skills enhancements necessary to become successful leaders in any work environment.

Enon Tabernacle Baptist Church—Philadelphia, Pennsylvania (senior pastor: Dr. Alyn E. Waller)

Enon Tabernacle, founded in 1876, was the first Black Baptist church in the Germantown section of Philadelphia. It sponsors over 60 ministries. The church has adopted the Mercy Home of Children orphanage in Uganda. Its international partnership in Kenya with Keiyo Soy Ministries provides water, education, and spiritual support. The Community Reinvestment Ministry invests in programs that address: the elderly; homelessness; education; youth; health prevention and wellness; arts and culture; and, evangelism and mission. The church redistributes 10 percent of its tithes and offerings back into the community via grants and awards. In 2007, over $650,000 were donated.

Educational Highlights

Pastor Waller initiated the Sexual Abuse Survivor Ministry (SAS) in 2006 to provide a confidential, caring, safe space for survivors of sexual abuse and trauma to discuss their experiences and ways to heal through a faith experience. The ministry is open to males and females, ages 18 years and older, from the church and community. The seven-week program includes two-hour meetings held twice monthly. Other activities provided during SAS include pastoral-led bible studies, breakout sessions, and journaling to address topics such as forgiveness, self-esteem, releasing toxic emotions and behavior, and anger redirection. If needed, external referrals are available. The overall program goal is to transition a person from "victim" to "victor." In addition to Christian summer camp and year-round childcare services, Enon provides over 40 children and youth programs. A variety of choral and musical options are available for children as young as three years old. In particular, the church's Drummers for Christ and Ordered Steps step team rival similar college-level performers. Enon is currently developing the Alliance for the Development of Human Potential (ADHP) non-profit organization that will serve as a reentry and job creation program. One of its arms will include employment such as landscaping and janitorial services for at-risk community members; another subsidiary will include business ventures.

The Greater Allen A.M.E. Cathedral of New York—Jamaica Queens, New York (co-pastors: Drs. Floyd and Elaine Flake)

Organized in 1893, Greater Allen has over 23,000 members and assets of over $92 million. It is the largest congregation in New York State. Its *One Choice, One Voice: Abstinence until Marriage Project* is a 50-week teen program that includes courses on self-esteem, self-development, values, goals, family diversity, and sexuality. Via multiple CDCs, the church has built about 225 two-family homes and refurbished over 300 units. Its multi-service center, the only one of its kind in the Queens borough, houses a clinic, mental health and counseling center, parenting skills programs for teenagers, and a center for geriatric and pediatric patients.

Educational Highlights

Greater Allen spearheads one of the top 10 ranked Head Start programs in the country and is the first church to partner with the *Princeton Review* to provide on-site test preparation courses for high school juniors and seniors as well as LSAT, GMAT, and GRE exams. It is the only church in the nation that offers this full spectrum of *Princeton Review* courses. Via church collaboration with local agencies and Queens College/CUNY's "Women and Work Program," women learn job skills and strategies to preempt domestic violence. In 2007 alone, efforts helped place 23 percent of its families into permanent housing. In 1992, the co-pastors organized the Shekinah Youth Church. With a current membership of over 1,100 youth, it has been recognized as a model for youth-directed church programming in the United States. In addition to religious programs, college fairs and tours are spearheaded via the College Preparation and Enrichment Program (CPEP). The Fashion Ministry (FM) sponsors workshops on appropriate attire for worship, school, and work. Persons can expand their biblical knowledge through the 15-course offerings at the Cathedral Bible Institute (CBI). Through a partnership between Nyack College and the church that began in 2003, persons with 60 or more college credit hours can complete their undergraduate degree and also earn a graduate degree on-site in the Adult Degree Completion Program.

Greater Mt. Calvary Holy Church—Washington, D.C. (co-pastors Bishop Alfred Owens Jr. and Rev. Susie Owens)

Greater Mt. Calvary, the largest Pentecostal church in the Washington, D.C., area, was founded in 1966 by its pastor with seven members in a storefront; it now has a membership of over 6,000. The Bishop Alfred A. Owens Jr. Family Life Center is a state-of-the art recreation and training facility opened in 2000 to provide wholesome alternatives to urban residents. In the "heart of Ward 5," it features a 300-seat auditorium, weight and fitness room, game room, saunas, a dance studio, Internet-accessable computer lab, kid's sports room, barbershop with barber and hairstylist, and classrooms. The facility is also unique because of its four-lane bowling alley and rooftop regulation-size basketball and tennis court. Counseling services, GED classes, entrepreneurial and professional development programs, recreational activities, and youth drug prevention programs are held at the Family Life Center.

Educational Highlights

Greater Mt. Calvary provides employment training, job referral services, and holistic programs including alcohol and drug counseling, health education, and educational referral services for at-risk youth. The ICAA-accredited Bible Institute and Christian academy extend formal education to both adults and children. In *Memorable Moments*, co-pastor Susie Owens (2003) underscores the church's emphasis on self-efficacy, personal pride, initiative, and empowerment:

> You cannot walk to the next level God is taking this church if you are scared. Folks are going to talk about us. 'Who do they think they are over there—in—in the ghetto? Who do they think they are?....You've got to have courage to believe in yourself, to stay strong, and to walk with God, so when the promises of God are released, you are right in line. (P. 28)

Mt. Calvary was one of the first Black churches to formally respond to HIV/AIDS in the Black community. Since 1983, it has provided an extensive federally funded HIV/AIDS program including: free, confidential alcohol and drug intervention and prevention programs using spiritual principles; clinical treatment; anger management classes; counseling; emergency food, clothing, housing, and transportation services; treatment program referrals; abstinence programs; a 12-step program; and, counseling and referrals for persons who experience depression. CATAADA House (Calvary's Alternative to Alcohol and Drug Abuse) provides about 10–15 intakes and 200 program services weekly; participant progress and outcomes are monitored monthly via program alumni and a tracking team.

Metropolitan Baptist Church—Washington, D.C. (senior servant: Dr. H. Beecher Hicks Jr.)

Metropolitan was organized by 10 persons in 1864. Today, the church's subsidiary corporations, commercial ventures, and over 50 ministries employ about 100 persons. The Garment's Hem, Inc. provides medical and mental health programs such as individual and family therapy, counseling, crisis intervention, and drug and alcohol prevention and treatment. The church's CDC is a 501c3 non-profit corporation that focuses on community outreach and improvement through education, real estate development, and health and human services. Metropolitan also has a partnership with Delta Sigma Theta Sorority Inc. focused on adult education. Since 1956, the church has also sponsored a credit union and is one of the first churches in Washington, D.C., to have a ministry dedicated to AIDS.

Educational Highlights

Even as early as 1883, the church's membership was about 1,500 and its emphasis on education was evident when it instituted Kiddie Kollege, a night school to teach Blacks to read and write. Its first Day School was organized in 1880 with 40 children. The Day School, incorporated in 1998, currently has enrolled about 1,000 students from Pre-K to 6th grade. In 2005–06, about 31 of the students were funded through the Opportunity Scholarship Program and the Washington Scholarship Fund. Small classes, state-of-the-art-technology, a Christian environment, academic and performance-based curriculum, a homework center, as well as after-school classes in African drum, piano, sewing, and basketball provide an alternative to under-funded local public schools. The Day School's over $350,000 mortgage was paid in full in 2005. In addition, the Christian Discipleship Institute provides biblical and practical courses for children and adults including caregiving classes, a Men's Academy, Servant Leadership seminars, age-specific bible studies, and counseling.

New Birth Missionary Baptist Church—Atlanta, Georgia (senior pastor: Bishop Eddie L. Long)

With origins back to 1939, New Birth is one of the largest churches in the country. The over 250-acre campus consists of a $50 million complex and over 25,000 members. It sponsors over 40 ministries as well as international evangelism programs. The Employment Ministry provides job listings, job fairs, and career development courses. Skills development activities focus on strategic job searches, résumé creation, and job search assistance. An Evangelism Ministry spearheads "Feed the Homeless" programs and neighborhood cleanup efforts.

Educational Highlights

During its 15-week program, the NXLEVEL Entrepreneur Training

Institute teaches participants the skill sets needed to establish viable businesses. The New Birth Christian Academy provides accredited, holistic development for students Pre-K through 12th grade. Students are exposed to courses in performing arts, music, computers, foreign languages, and Kingdom theology. New Birth also hosts educational and inspirational conferences that include internationally and nationally known speakers, breakout sessions, and praise and worship periods. Heart to Heart Women's Conference focuses on parenting, marriage, health, and finances; the Men's Conference addresses leadership, marriage, entrepreneurship, overcoming addictions, and health; and the Singles Conference centers the single experience, finances, relationships, spiritual guidance, and health. Other conferences include the Spirit and Truth Conference for church leaders and The Movement for youth ages 9–18 years. In response to an increase in the local Hispanic population, the church organized, New Birth Latino. In addition to offering Spanish classes, bilingual services are held each Sunday at 2:30 p.m.

Pentecostal Church of Christ—Cleveland, Ohio (co-pastors: Bishop J. Delano and Dr. Sabrina Ellis)

Founded in 1935, the Pentecostal COC is the oldest Pentecostal congregation in Cleveland and the "Mother Church" of apostolic assemblies throughout Cuyahoga County. Bishop Ellis has served as senior pastor since 1989; his wife, Rev. Ellis is the Overseer (pastor). In addition to his pastoral role, in 1989, Bishop J. Ellis established and organized the United Pentecostal Churches of Christ (COC) in which he now serves as President of the Joint College of African American Pentecostal Bishops. According to the senior pastor, "we believe we have been called to lead God's people back to unrestrained praise and to life in the name of Jesus." Pentecostal COC's radio program, "Sound of Pentecost," has broadcasted for over 20 years and its newsletter, *The Shepherd's Voice*, is published weekly. The Missionary and Benevolence Ministry responds to community needs through food and clothing donations and sick visitation.

Educational Highlights

In 1990, the church purchased a local office building (renamed the J.D. Ellis Plaza) that now houses Christian Education classrooms, a Sacristy, and office space. Through partnerships with local agencies, the church provides spiritual and financial support, volunteers, employment information, and other resources to poor and homeless people in the Cleveland area.

Ray of Hope Christian Church—Atlanta, Georgia (senior pastor: Dr. Cynthia Hale)

Ray of Hope was founded in 1986 by four persons and currently has an active membership of over 3,500. Prior to becoming a pastor, Dr. Hale served as the first female chaplain at an all-male federal correctional facility. The church currently has about 50 ministries and has been recognized as one of the 300 excellent Protestant churches in the United States in the book, *Excellent Protestant Congregations: The Guide to Best Places and Practice*. As of 2006, Pastor Hale is the Necrologist for the Hampton Ministers Conference. Locally known as "The Ray," the church supports a mobile clinic that provides healthcare and support to the under-serviced.

Educational Highlights

The Hope Institute for Christian Discipleship (HICD) provides formal Christian education, builds spiritual intimacy, and promotes leadership through intensive classes held during winter, spring, and fall sessions. Its programs encourage gender inclusivity by intentionally creating spaces where both men and women are empowered and supportive of each other. The Daughters of Destiny Ministry develops annual thematic activities for women. For example, the 2007 foci were health, relationships, business, and wealth addressed during quarterly sessions and a national women's conference. Complementary programs such as the "Man on Fire Movement" meet each Monday and outings via Brothers in the Hood Night provide wholesome, creative outlets for men. Youth programs such as XTREME Takeover, Jump Off, and College Hill sponsor activities, community outreach, and fellowship for persons aged 13–25 years.

Salem Baptist Church—Chicago, Illinois (senior pastor: Rev. James T. Meeks)

Salem B.C. was organized in 1985 by 193 persons. It is now the largest church in Illinois with a membership of over 22,000 persons. Since 2003, Pastor Meeks has been a member of the Illinois Senate, representing the 15th district, and Chairperson of the Illinois Legislative Black Caucus. He also serves as Executive Vice President of the National Rainbow-PUSH Coalition. Since 2005, worship services have been held in a $50 million worship and multi-purpose facility. Via the "Adopt a Block" program, church volunteers walk door-to-door taking requests from residents for assistance ranging from food to basic home repairs. Most requests are filled and completed the following week. In 1999, the church spearheaded a citywide proselytizing campaign that resulted in over 29,000 persons accepting Christ. Salem has provided free HIV/AIDS screening since 1994 and its non-profit HIV/AIDS clinic is now in its second year. In 2007, Salem sponsored 21 weeks of free HIV/AIDS testing that costs an estimated $500,000. In 1998, the church organized a movement to dry up their community and collected votes that led to the closing of 26 neighborhood liquor stores. The pastor's following comment reflects a megachurch understanding of godly living and community engagement: "in order for the world to see how big God is, the world is going to have to see God's people doing God-sized things." In addition to revitalizing a poor urban space, the new worship center is available to church and community members for programs and activities.

Educational Highlights

Concerned about subpar public education in inner-city spaces, the church established the Salem Christian Academy (SCA) in 1990. The current enrollment of 500 students, Pre-K through 8th grade, receives biblically based education. The church also sponsored the largest deputy training drive in the county (Chicago Board of Election volunteer Deputy Registrar Program classes). The "It Takes a Village" program provides mentoring for pregnant girls and young mothers. Additionally, because segments of the Black population are less likely to donate organs, but more likely to need them, Salem spearheaded the largest organ donation drive in the county.

St. Stephen Baptist Church—Louisville, Kentucky (senior pastor: Dr. Kevin W. Cosby)

St. Stephen was organized in 1926 by 14 members. It now has a membership of over 10,000. Dr. Kevin Cosby became pastor in 1979 at the age of 20. In 1993, a $1.4 million, 1,600 seat worship center was built. Yet it was inadequate given the approximately 1,700 person attendance during Wednesday Night bible service and 7,000 persons during weekend worship services. A $5 million, 1,000 seat church/prayer retreat center was built and, in 2001, the Family Life Center was renovated to include two basketball courts, a bookstore, a café, racquetball courts, saunas, a dance studio, a state-of-the-art fitness center, and classroom space that can accommodate 2,500 people. St. Stephen was recognized in 2005 by *Outreach Magazine* as one of the top 100 largest churches in America and in *Emerge Magazine* as one of the six super churches of the South. In addition to midweek bible studies, five worship services are held—a Saturday and three Sunday services at the Louisville campus and a Sunday morning service as the south Indiana campus.

Educational Highlights

In 2005, a transitional house for recovering addicts was opened. The facility, called Hotel California, houses 16 men for periods of up to one year during which they participate in life-coping activities, 12-step programs, mentoring, and self-esteem workshops. The church's emphasis on social justice as well as community and individual empowerment are reflected in the pastor's challenge to "serve God in the midst of social oppression." According to the pastor, St. Stephen provides instruction "from GED to PhD." In addition to a high school equivalency program, the church recently purchased Simmons College, a Christian institution of higher education, and restored it to its initial stature on the original site. Founded by slaves, it is one of the first municipally owned colleges in the state. It is also one of the oldest Black-owned and -operated colleges in the nation. Pastor Cosby serves as college president.

Trinity United Church of Christ—Chicago, Illinois (senior pastor: Rev. Otis Moss and pastor emeritus: Dr. Jeremiah Wright)

In December 1961, 123 people took part in its first worship service. Now Trinity has over 8,500 active members. The stained-glass windows in the main sanctuary have an estimated value of almost $4 million and depict biblical scenes as well as stories and persons associated with Africa and Africans in the Diaspora such as Christ feeding the 5,000, the Crucifixion and Resurrection of Christ, Tutankhamen, Nefertari, Moses and Zipporah, St. Phillip, Cyprian, Revs. Richard Allen and Nanny Helen Burroughs, Harriet Tubman, and Dr. William Faulkner. The church has five separate corporations that sponsor programs and activities seven days and week, 365 days of the year. These include three childcare programs, two senior citizen housing complexes, and a 70-family apartment complex. Their senior housing has been nationally recognized as a model for low-income residency. Trinity also sponsors a federally chartered credit union. The Community Health Corporation oversees the church's counseling center, Hospice Care Ministry, nationally recognized HIV/AIDS Ministry, and a Health and Wellness ministry.

Educational Highlights

The church's motto is "Unashamedly Black and Unapologetically Christian." Education, health and wellness, counseling, and daycare programs are housed at the church's second campus. Trinity sponsors over 70 ministries, including over 22 different programs specifically for youth, 25 weekly adult bible classes, and its own bookstore. Its Kwame Nkrumah Academy provides Afro-centered instruction to youth in classes K–6. The church embraces a Black Value System that emphasizes commitment to God, the Black community, the Black family, self-discipline and self-respect, Black institutions, the pursuit of excellence, and the disavowal of the pursuit of "middle-classness." It also sponsors an annual High School College Fair that highlights HBCUs, at least four annual college tours for juniors and seniors, and extensive financial aid for seminarians. Its Center for African Biblical Studies focuses on the study of the bible from an African perspective.

Victory Church—Atlanta, Georgia (senior pastor: Dr. Kenneth L. Samuel)

Organized in 1987 by its pastor, Victory Church has a nationwide reputation as a welcoming and affirming church for all persons. Ordained at age 23 at the Ebenezer Baptist Church in Atlanta, Pastor Samuel has been elected as a Georgia delegate to the last four Democratic National conventions. In 2002, the current 3,000-seat worship center was completed on 25 acres. It includes a 500-seat fellowship hall, classrooms, a library, a bookstore, administrative offices, and a recording studio. The Kenneth L. Samuel Community Life Center, also located on the main campus, houses a full court gymnasium, classrooms, a computer lab, and office space. In addition to sponsoring Meals on Wheels and Project Open Hand, the church spearheads a Food and Clothing Bank Ministry that has been in place about 15 years and services 25–30 families a month.

Educational Highlights

The Victory Christian Academy serves K- through 5th grade. The church's 50-person volunteer staff, Victory over HIV/AIDS Ministry, provides one-on-one counseling, seminars, spiritual support, conferences, education material, and community outreach. Free and confidential AIDS testing is performed each Thursday. The program is lauded for its creative approaches to encourage testing. For example, February 7, 2007, the ministry organized and hosted an HIV/AIDS concert at the church called "Your Test Is Your Ticket" where taking part in free, confidential testing was the "entrance fee." The concert featured gospel recording artists Byron Case and Detrick Hadden. Over 5,000 persons (including 1,000 church members) were tested as a result of the concert efforts. Other education-related ministries include Jesus and Me (J.A.M.) Youth Church and an after-school program.

Victory Church of Nashville, Tennessee (senior pastor: Bishop Kenneth H. Dupree)

Founded in 1989 by the pastor and 21 persons, Victory is a multicultural congregation. Bishop Dupree has been preaching since the age of 12. An accomplished singer, he toured with the Charles Fold Singers and earned a Grammy award while singing with the group. His latest CD is entitled, "Melodies and Messages for Conquerors." The church's radio broadcast, "Living in Victory," for which he is Executive Producer, has a listening audience of over 60,000. Through the Victory Empowerment Center, the church recently purchased 86 acres of land for the development of Victory Estates, over 300 upscale single- and multi-family homes, assisted living facilities, a golf range, as well as a community center. It is considered the largest land development of its kind in the state of Tennessee. The pastors' ministry of victorious living emphasizes lifestyle changes through Christian instruction and personal empowerment:

> People are important, and relationships are important and love is important, connecting with people is important. You can't go through life detached, unconcerned, self centered, self-seeking. We have to care about people. As we learn to love God, love ourselves, we can love others. And be taught to love life—to live. There's a world out there to see. There are dolphins to be swum with, mountains to be climbed, oceans to be swum in, books to be read and songs to be heard. And if you don't know that, I'm here to teach you, 'Hey, come on.' I want to break the curse of poverty…change the way you think, change the way you live.

Educational Highlights

About 20 percent of the church's annual income is used to support efforts such as the annual Back-to-School Bash that equips at least 100 children with school supplies; drug rehabilitation programs led by former users; and college scholarships. Youth programs target education and awareness via topics such as sexual awareness, condom use, and self-esteem. The Victory Housing Counseling Center was established to educate persons about home-ownership. It has assisted over 400 families, primarily single mothers, in becoming home-owners. Victory Academy offers Saturday classes for all ages from 10:00 a.m. to 12:00 p.m.

Program and Ministry Impact Typology

Figure 5.1 provides a typology of many of the programs sponsored by the churches profiled here and their potential impact. Particular attention is given to education-related endeavors. The schematic is informative on several fronts. First, it provides a broad overview of Black megachurch best practices. Second, readers are able to visualize how certain programs possibly overlap, intersect, or are actually disconnected from others in terms of scope and potential outcomes. And lastly, it is possible to consider the degree to which Black megachurch educational offerings have promise to affect change at micro- and macro-levels. The typology is purposely situated within the structure versus agency discourse because this framework allows a critical assessment of whether and how individual choice and systemic forces influence outcomes. Many sociological debates concerning inequalities and other social problems have been referenced using cultural exemplars (i.e., agency) versus structural ones. Thus one can ask whether, given their considerable resources and unique features, Black megachurch programs to educate, equip, and empower are driven by goodwill and the desire to meet pressing individual, more short-term problems? Or are they more justice oriented with a focus toward social transformation and societal reform? Simply put, if Black megachurches are forces to be reckoned with, is it reasonable to reckon that their traditional and nontraditional educational efforts are working to dismantle negative structural forces? Or, despite their expansive nature and impressive formats, are their programs largely priestly with an emphasis on individual initiative and self-efficacy?

Programs are grouped within and across four quadrants based on their micro- or macro-level possible effects as well as whether they represent traditional forms of benevolence or address broader systemic issues of social justice (i.e., more short- or long-term remedies). Readers will notice that worship and religious education programs are included in every group to remind readers of the biblical impetus for most efforts. It should also be noted that certain programs reflect both structure and agency and cannot be pigeon-holed in terms of impetus or outcomes. For example, employment programs and skills training workshops can provide important immediate and long-term positive effects; they may also be spearheaded because of a church's desire to affect both individual and collective good. However, other programs can more easily be placed in (and across) certain quadrants. The goal here is not to over-generalize the potential impact of Black megachurch offerings, but rather to consider different forms of transformation that can result.

Programs in Group A tend to be much more focused on benevolence and meeting individual needs; many are subsistence related. Their possible systemic impact is minimal, but evident when one considers the collective effects if large numbers of people avail themselves of such programs. Activities and ministries in Group B intersect across all four quadrants suggesting their more varied foci and potential impact. Several are tangentially linked to education (for example, providing 150-unit low-cost apartments), but respond to larger group needs and help people meet basic concerns such that training and instruction are more tenable. Others seem more individualistic (for example, day- and after-care), but their absence undermines self-efficacy and upward mobility for a disproportionate percentage of Blacks, especially single mothers and working-class families.[6] Although these programs directly impact skill sets and personal capacity, I distinguish them from the latter group because, save Christian Education programs, most do not typically occur daily. Yet some programs overlap with those in the last group. However, long-term effects are possible if large numbers of people are impacted (for example, the effects on local urban neighborhoods of job placement programs).

Programs in Group C extend the efforts found in the previous group; tend to be larger in scale and scope; usually provide offerings to increased numbers of people; and are often tied to secular alliances and networks outside the church. Most of these programs coincide with economic, political, and social problems directly or indirectly related to education. It is likely that placement of certain programs will result in debate—should advocacy programs be included in Group C rather than Group B? How is capacity-building distinct from certain educational programs in Group C? Furthermore, inter-church variation exists. For example, for several churches, HIV preventions/interventions can be included in Group C because of the large number of services that are continually offered. The schematic is expected to generate candid conversations about how Black megachurch programs actually impact the congregants and communities they purport to serve. The typology illustrates the self-help tradition found among Black megachurches as well as their cafeteria-style programs—even when only considering education-related options. Although these programs position people to better and more successfully live, few efforts appear to directly confront structural forces or attempt to dismantle them systemically.

Conclusion

Common problems in Black communities have resulted in common programs across Black megachurches such as food and clothing programs, prison ministries, niche-specific social support, family-oriented events, and activities for children and youth. Similarly, spiritual-based and administrative efforts such as Christian Education, greeters, elders, trustees, deacons, and nurses are in place. Most pastors and co-pastors are formally trained, published, and speak and lecture internationally and nationally. Cafeteria-style programs are the norm; the majority of Black megachurches here are full-service institutions that provide programs and ministries seven days a week, 24 hours a day. However, programs are variable and reflect the unique character of each congregation and leadership as well as the specific challenges congregants and local residents face. In the Black megachurch environment, activities often associated with secular spaces such as dances, theatre, corporations, bands, ice-cream parlors, youth step and drum teams are appropriated, expanded, and influenced by Christian tenets, Black traditions in general, and Black Church cultural tools specifically—some more directly and others because of locale. Ministries and acronym-named programs reflect wholesome, creative alternatives to attract upper- and middle-class families, young urban Black professionals as well as their counterparts who aspire to emulate them.

These church profiles illustrate just how Black megachurches can become proxies for secular organizations, affiliations, and experiences when they reflect community-, race-, and in some instances, class-specific endeavors that target and respond to persons who are diverse in their aspirations and accomplishments, concerned about familial and personal challenges, exposed to social injustices, and who have high expectations from the congregations where they worship. For many congregants, Black megachurch programs are substantially more attractive than their secular counterparts because they reflect Christian tenets and wholesome objectives and take place in church-controlled spaces. Such programs are also tangible evidence of favor, self-efficacy, accountability, and power.

The historic Black Church has been one of few institutions owned and controlled by Blacks; so too is the Black megachurch. A strong argument can be made that the latter institutions wield considerably more relative power today than their predecessors given their access to contemporary spaces prevented by racial segregation in the past. The influence afforded Black megachurches can translate into collective power and increased positive self-identity for congregants and community residents who seek their services. Additionally, access to multiple worship experiences, ministries, and programs enable people to choose concerted involvement, selective anonymity, or something in between.[7] Yet regardless of their level of engagement, most people can still avail themselves of the programs such churches have to offer. But by doing so, they begin to take part in some of the very processes that ultimately engender consistent participation.[8] Church-based alternatives to secular programs are not new in the Black religious tradition. DuBois (1903[2003]) chronicled this tendency decades ago in *The Negro Church*. What makes Black megachurch dynamics different is the scope and creativity of their efforts and the intense message of self-actualization that appears to attract masses.

Regardless of church age, pastoral profile, denomination, or locale, the Black megachurches profiled here sponsor traditional and nontraditional educational programs. In doing so, they illustrate that education and empowerment can take place through assorted mechanisms. In addition to offering priestly activities, most understand their role as prophetic institutions in the Black community and larger society. Although benevolence is apparent, programmatic efforts often include a social justice component; personal capacity building; strategic alliances; instrumental and expressive responses to short- and long-term challenges; and systemic, formulaic instructions on how to experience upward mobility. Despite diverse church goals, the broad objective is to establish, reinforce, and codify the relationship between godly, victorious living, self-efficacy, and intra-church connectedness.

As described by Swidler (1986), the churches studied here take advantage of existing cultural tools that work, but ratchet them up in scope such that extreme messages of empowerment become embedded in the nature and scope of programs. Formal educational processes occur through schools, workshops, forums, certificate and degree programs, both secular and spiritual, as well as affiliations with long-standing national testing centers that have largely benefited the White community. Somewhat more subliminal, but consistent messages of success are sprinkled throughout worship, meetings, and other instances when two or three gather. These courses of action are infused with Black Church cultural tools such as self-help and linked fate beliefs as well as Black megachurch cultural components tied to favor and "Kingdom Building." They combine tried and true instructional processes and practices with an unconventional understanding of how God can and does work in the lives of the faithful. By doing so, intangible cultural components combined with godly validation and structured learning spaces work to create formidable systems to educate and empower.

Figure 5.1 Typology of Black Megachurch Educational Programs and Their Potential Impact (N=16)

AGENCY

Group A
Christian education/Worship
Food/Clothing
Counseling
Conventions/Forums/Workshops
Drug abuse/Sexuality courses

BENEVOLENCE

Group B
Christian education/Worship
Real estate
College tours
Advocacy/Job placement
Capacity-building programs
HIV prevention/intervention

SOCIAL JUSTICE

STRUCTURE

Group C
Christian education/Worship
Day schools/Academies
Literacy/GED/Job training programs
Computer courses
College extension programs
Kaplan/Standardized test programs
Prison re-entry programs
Day- and After-care
Tutoring
CDCs
Health/Health education clinics
Lobbying

Key:
Programs/ministries not listed in any order and do not reflect the totality of programs offered by the sample churches. *Christian education includes religious-education programs such as Sunday school and bible studies. Capacity-building includes formal, but less systemically enmeshed programs such as periodic niche-specific programs. Real estate refers to large-scale projects that house large numbers of persons/families (included in Group B rather than Group C because they are indirectly related to educational programs). Advocacy reflects large-scale job placement, social policy action, and mobilization to combat inequality. CDCs refer to Community Development Corporations (included because most educational programs among sample churches are spearheaded via such corporations).

Notes

1. Each profile was developed by reviewing survey data, church histories, bulletins, interviewing clergy and members, reading books written by pastors, listening to sermon tapes by pastors, locating newspaper articles, scouring church pamphlets, magazines, and websites, taking church tours, and engaging in participant observation at each site. When necessary, interview quotes and direct observation results are included to complement each profile. Profiles were written by this author, who takes responsibility for potential inconsistencies and inaccuracies. The objective is not to duplicate information found on church websites or in their histories but to highlight creative educational offerings.

2. SAMM is a culturally competent program designed to reduce HIV-risk behavior. This goal is accomplished through a partnership with the AIDS Taskforce of Greater Cleveland, Cleveland Public Schools, concerned teenagers throughout Greater Cleveland, and community organizations.

3. It has been estimated that at least half of all new HIV infections in the United States are among people under the age of 25. The average current time from initial HIV infection to a clinical diagnosis of AIDS of 11 years, suggests that many AIDS cases represent HIV infections that occurred during young adult years. Furthermore, the HIV infection rate for Black Cleveland youth is 30 times the statewide average.

4. Rupon (2007: A1, A9).

5. Fulton (2007: B7–8).

6. A large body of literature supports this point (Anderson and Van Hoy 2006; Barnes 2004; Billingsley 1992; Edin and Lein 1996; Fellmeth 2005; Jarrett 1994; Peck and Segal 2006; Shipler 2004; Stack 1974; Wijnberg and Weinger 1998; Wilson 1996).

7. Schaller (1990).

8. Schaller (1990) also suggests that megachurches can provide so many programs because a larger relative percent of their funds are available for programs. Additionally, the base of volunteers of megachurches is substantially larger than that found in smaller churches.

Conclusion

Black Megachurches and the Future

Continuing to Create Culture

According to Lincoln and Mamiya (1990), "no other area of Black life received a higher priority from Black churches than education" (p. 251). Findings in this book suggest that this legacy continues among the Black megachurches examined here, but often in inventive ways. The leadership and membership of these large congregations think and behave "outside the box" because, as members of God's elect, they believe they *can* and *should*—and because they *must* if they expect to attain both their specific church and personal goals and objectives. For most, traditionalism can result in constraints on creativity and limited thinking that ultimately undermine the very nature of a church's stance. I am not suggesting a panacea—readers should not consider Black megachurches to be perfect. Like any institution or group of people, they have flaws, limitations, and areas in need of improvement. However, as chronicled by the mystic and scholar Howard Thurman, I argue that prophetic Black megachurch leaders are able to concretize a spiritual message where "a built-in sense of the Creator provides oppressed people with ultimate meaning and the ability to transform circumstances" (Cannon 1988: 160). However, these pastors do not consider themselves or their followers oppressed because of godly favor and radical expectations. And the drive that emanates from such an extreme spiritual stance becomes contagious when evident and consistently emphasized during varied church experiences. This means pastors are able to sloth off the troubling context and parameters of Thurman's observations and focus on his announcement that "there is always something that can be done about anything" (as quoted in Cannon 1988: 162). Such beliefs require an indomitable spirit and goal of excellence found when the Black Church is at its best.[1]

Just as scholars make reference to "Black Church culture,"[2] it is appropriate to do the same when describing the Black megachurch. Although much of this analysis identifies ways in which culture found in these large institutions reflects a fusion of other cultural traditions, it is evident that Black megachurches also create their own cultural traditions. Even re-imagined, re-appropriations of past cultural tools constitute new cultural expressions. However, it is important to continue to identify and acknowledge those cultural tools unique to Black megachurches. Although some of them have been identified in this book, continued efforts are needed to uncover other innovative meanings, motivations, and programs these institutions employ to education, empower, and solidify their own niches in the religious terrain. I believe that part of the investigative process will require researchers to broaden the definition of a *megachurch*. Current definitions are woefully inadequate in understanding and defining the Black megachurch phenomenon. Terms such as the "giga church" are now in use; additional ways of operationalizing such churches are in order. The findings in this analysis beg for new definitions that consider features other than mean worship attendance and take into consideration the quality and quantity of both church-community involvement and programmatic offerings. Varied definitions that blur traditional boundaries should also consider outcomes and religious styles (for example, priestly vs. prophetic). Thumma and Travis (2007) provide a strong start in this regard, but do not focus on the Black religious experience. Scholars able to do the latter will provide a unique contribution to the study of religiosity, theology, social movements, and the Black experience.

My findings show that several profiled churches are more internally focused, concentrate efforts on spiritual programs, and are only more recently venturing into concerted community service. The forte of several others appears to be conventions and forums; yet relative to their size, they are not as actively engaged in community outreach programs as some of the "smaller" megachurches. And some congregations are not involved in any international efforts. These types of church features and cultural markers should be taken into consideration when defining a church as "mega." Fruitful discussion and collaborations would emerge between scholars and clergy (many of the latter are formally trained with Doctor of Ministry degrees). I initially selected a sample based on church "size". But for several churches, the definition extended beyond a traditional one as I became intrigued by innovative programs, creative activities, sustained community involvement, magnitude and range of ministries relative to the *city size*, as well as impact in light of church size. The nature and scope of Black megachurch educational programs is another important evaluative criterion. Public school inadequacies, the "Catholic School advantage," and efforts by the nine schools presented in this study, make a strong argument for the establishment of more such private schools. Both federal and state governments continue to look to schools to combat inequality; history suggests prudence in the Black community when expecting concerted reform from outside sources. Whether the onus for ameliorating social problems they did not create should fall on the shoulders of Black megachurches will require candid conversations between leadership and membership on subjects such as self-help, societal complicity, the role of race in contemporary spaces, and church callings. Conversations and continued interventions are crucial.

Readers should note that although this work is infused with pastoral commentary, these findings do not point to pastor's profile as a singular explanatory factor. I could have also concentrated on other issues, some of which will be addressed in my future studies on this subject. However, I was interested in education, broadly defined, and varied processes by which church culture is used to shape the minds and lives of believers. I attempted to provide details for a subset of Black megachurches to open a window into the daily and weekly mechanisms that result in a "mega mentality" among leaders and members. The goal was not all encompassing and the study limitations have been described earlier and in the appendix. The presence of Baptist and denominationally independent churches here is clear; these churches are disproportionately found among Black megachurches. Future studies should expand this sampling base by including more particularistic congregations. Moreover, a certain degree of self-selection is suggested among sample churches. Those congregations that aren't as involved in community action or that do not sponsor cafeteria programs may have been more reticent to participate in this project. Yet based on the range and scope of programs among these sample churches (and the relatively limited offerings of a few), this effect is believed to be minimal and did not undermine the research goals of locating and profiling a cross-section of the most common types of large Black churches.

Despite their considerable human and economic resources, it will be important to continue to assess the role and relevance of Black megachurches in society. A variety of race-related questions remain—such as their response to the "post-racial Obama" age. What does this statement mean for large Black churches? Will those that espouse a more race-neutral persona move further toward racial ambiguousness and sloth off remnants of Black Church culture for a much more color-blind congregation? Will more Black-identified congregations alter their posture or bear down further in their position? Will programs change if social policy and societal attitudes that "race no longer matters" undermine existing government-sponsored programs and services? Other queries are also important. Because several churches here sponsor clinics, it may not be a stretch to expect Black megachurch–run hospitals in the future as a response to continued healthcare inequities. What type of carbon footprint will large Black churches leave? Do certain pastors espouse loftier political aspirations? And given the premise of this project, how will the use of Black Church cultural tools fare during these dynamics? What new church cultural tools will emerge? Of equal merit will be correlates between economic challenges such as poverty, unemployment, healthcare reform, and housing inequities and the *messages* espoused in Black megachurches. One would expect the current recession to impact the message of favor and success—particularly for prosperity proponents.[3] It remains unclear whether it will be necessary to nuance this message or broaden it.

Answers remain to be seen, but can be expected to influence current as well as future Black megachurch cultural tools.

The majority of the profiled churches can be considered prophetic and intentionally sponsor programs in response to social problems that affect the Black community. Furthermore, most pastors are comfortable challenging the status quo and critiquing dimensions of society they believe undermine the spiritual and non-spiritual quality of life of believers. However, only a few clergy directly challenge capitalism as an economic system in a way that would suggest the need to dismantle systemic forces that perpetuate inequality. This latter assessment suggests the need to critically examine whether the considerable resources at the disposal of Black megachurches (and megachurches in general) are being harnessed in the best way to concertedly bring "God's Kingdom" to earth.

If, as Swidler (1986, 1995) suggests, groups tend to employ cultural tools shown to be effective in the past, the current successes of many Black megachurches may make it difficult to change in an ever-changing society. Issues associated with succession and alliances may be particularly susceptible to routinization. Although apparently open to change, innovation, and proactivity, if certain cultural tools work, why change them? However, the nature of the church socialization processes found in most of these congregations suggests spaces dynamic enough to effectively ride the ebbs and flows of the most tempestuous religious market. However, some type of Black megachurch alliance would seem expedient to harness the church capital they possess. Yet, according to the co-pastor of a Pentecostal church in this analysis, here lies the rub that she ascribes to the Christian tradition in general and Black churches in particular:

> Churches don't really come together for any cause. Black churches in particular…because everybody is possessive because, 'this is my thing' or 'these are my people.' I don't know what the fear is. But there's not a lot of comradery …this has been said forever, you can do more together than you can apart….There's not a lot a fellowship, you may have certain pockets, but not in general.

However, if the following more optimistic remarks from the pastor of a Baptist church in the Midwest about the prospects of an alliance are realized, considerably more efforts to educate and empower will emerge from Black megachurch spaces; "that would be beautiful. And megachurches can come and learn from each other."

Notes

1. Refer to the large literature in studies such as Barnes (2004, 2005, 2006), Billingsley (1999), Drake and Cayton (1940), Gilkes (2001), Higginbotham (1993), Lincoln (1984), Lincoln and Mamiya (1990), Mays and Nicholson (1933), McRoberts (2003), Morris (1984), West (1982), Wilmore (1994).
2. Barnes (2005), Pattillo-McCoy (1999).
3. Thompson (1999).

Appendix

Methodological Overview

THIS BOOK RELIES ON A MIXED METHODOLOGY using quantitative and qualitative data. A case study was performed for each of the 16 sample Black megachurches that included clergy in-depth interviews, survey data, pastors' sermons (video and audio), and participant observation data. In addition, Faith Factor 2000 and historical material from each congregation (primarily written, but some website information) were used as supporting information. In order to present the most comprehensive portrait of the social milieu under study, multi-methods are often suggested in sociological inquiry. In this instance, they are almost required to study the environments and programs of Black megachurches. Multiple data sources also enable a certain degree of cross-checking of self-reported data.

About the Qualitative Data

Interviews were performed with 16 clergy (n=16, 12 pastors and four clergy representatives). I interviewed pastors because pastors of Black churches have been shown to weld considerably more influence than their White counterparts (Lincoln and Mamiya 1990; McRoberts 2003). Logistics prevented me from doing so in four instances. However, the church representatives were selected by their respective pastors and were prepared and knowledgeable to answer my queries. Audiotapes of pastors' sermons for each of the 16 churches as well as 15 additional Black megachurch pastors were used to augment the interview data. Studying sermons by Black megachurch pastors was particularly important in broadening my understanding of how scriptural interpretation, a key component of Black Church culture, took place. I was also able to identify sermonic patterns and compare and contrast preaching styles. Because I was interested in how worship could be creatively used as an instructional space, sermons, as the culmination of the worship experience, provided an important opportunity to determine various preaching and teaching strategies. Furthermore, the second set of sermons broadened the sample to include additional locations, denominations, and church types with the intent to collect a substantial amount of Black megachurch data from churches in geographic areas where Black megachurches are concentrated. I analyzed over 50 pastors' sermons. In some instances, pastors provided a selection of sermons; in other cases, bookstore clerks or my primary church contact chose sermons based on my descriptions of the broad research topics. However, when selecting sermons from church websites, I chose sermons with titles that seemed interesting or related to the topics of study (for example, subjects related to social problems, victorious living, economics, overcoming life's challenges, prosperity issues). So although the sermon selection process is purposive in nature, it also reflects some variation.

Selecting the Sample Black Megachurches and Collecting Data

It is commonly suggested that there are about 120–150 Black megachurches in the United States. I used this range as a guide to select at least a 10 percent sample from this population. More is generally better in order to get a better portrait of the overall population. Using this guideline and in light of clergy logistical constraints, I focused on 16 churches. Congregations were chosen based on two megachurch definitions linked to church size and programmatic efforts (Thumma and Travis 2007; Schaller 2000). Save one congregation, churches have mean weekend worship attendance of at least 2,000 adults. Most of them significantly exceed this benchmark. Although one congregation does not consistently meet this definition, I elected to retain it in the sample because it reflects aspects of Schaller's (2000) definition of a large church. It also added to the overall denominational mix and, relative to its size, is involved in a substantial and diverse number of community outreach programs. Church rolls range from 1,375 to over 25,000 members. The following denominations are represented: Baptists (n= 8 churches), Non-denominational (n=3), AME (n=1), Church of Christ (n=1), Disciples of Christ (n=1), Holiness (n=1), and Pentecostal (n=1). One of the congregations is considered Baptist but it is also affiliated with the Church of Christ. I included it in the Baptist category, but one might argue that it is largely non-denominational. I made initial contact by identifying, locating, and calling the pastor's administrative assistant(s). I mailed each church an informational packet about the project and samples of my published writing about the Black Church and poverty. A variety of e-mails and subsequent telephone calls and messages were sent during the process. Approximately 3–6 months elapsed between my initial contact and a pastor's decision to participate. The entire research project lasted about four years.

It was not the objective of this project to generalize findings based on 16 Black megachurches, but rather to include diverse congregations across denominations, pastor's gender, class mix, location, and pastor's profile. I also sought churches from locations where a larger proportion of Black megachurches are located such as Georgia, Illinois, Florida, Texas, California, and New York. Black megachurches from each of these areas, except Texas and Florida, are included in the sample of 16. I made numerous unsuccessful attempts to gain access to churches from these two locales. However, for a variety of reasons, pastors from churches in these two states elected not to participate in the study. In order to compensate, to some degree, for these exclusions, I studied the sermons from Black megachurch pastors from Texas, Florida, and other areas where Black megachurches are located. In terms of leadership, one church has a female pastor and four have husband and wife co-pastors.

Several comments are in order regarding self-selection. As expected, some pastors declined to take part in the project. Most decisions were due to scheduling problems; several were completing their own memoirs. However, several refused and no reason was provided. It is possible that those churches and pastors who believed that their church programs and stances would be seen in the best light would also be more apt to take part in the study. In contrast, Black megachurches with limited programs, especially relative to their sizes, might be less inclined to participate. However, program sponsorship and church profiles differ substantially across the 16 congregations. Thus I believe that self-selection is not a huge concern. It may also be possible that pastors were leery to take part because of past negative media coverage about megachurches. Others may have been concerned about the topics of study. I cannot determine the rationale of the non-participating churches. However, it is important to discuss the broad implications of these issues. I reference the most detailed analysis of the Black megachurch phenomena to consider some possible implications. Tucker (2002) suggests that Black megachurches tend to be located in cities such as Houston, Dallas, Atlanta, and Los Angeles. The latter two locales are represented in this study and pastoral sermons were reviewed from Black megachurches from all four areas. She also contends that the top 10 areas with the greatest number of Black megachurches as locations such as Washington, D.C., New York, Atlanta, Los Angeles, and Houston. Churches from the majority of these areas are part of my purposive sample. Furthermore, over one-fourth of Black megachurches are located in Washington, D.C., and Atlanta—areas represented in this analysis.

Participant Observation Process

Participant observation at each church site occurred over at least a 2- to 3-day period. I was able to tour surrounding neighborhoods and witness some of the inner-workings of the programs and ministries such as their academies/schools, poverty programs, family life centers, HIV/AIDS outreach programs, bookstores, drug-treatment centers, community recreational facilities and gymnasiums, children's and youth churches, food and clothing stores, drug rehabilitation centers, credit unions, and apartment complexes. I also had the opportunity to interview some of the leaders of church ministries. However, because I could not consistently interview leaders from these programs at each church site, their direct comments are not included in this analysis. I also engaged in participant observation during Sunday worship services. Readers should be cognizant of the limitations of using participant observation techniques. The reliability of data relies heavily on the training of the researcher. Some methodologists recommend using multiple observers to help increase reliability (Babbie 2002; Bickman and Rog 1998). However, in light of my past research experience observing church settings, the small sample size, the use of a consistent observation template by a single observer, and the focus on a specific set of church activities such as worship and church programs, I am confident in the observations that were uncovered as well as my analysis of them. For example, the goal was not to capture every nuance of a worship service, but to concentrate on the same, primary events across the Black megachurches such that comparisons and contrasts could be made. I attended multiple worship services. During each service, I assessed the overall worship style (for example, traditional or more contemporary); sermonic focus; scriptural use; worship leadership format (praise leader, deacons, choir, praise team, soloists); presence of call-and-response; use of dance; and types of songs included. In some instances, I was also able to attend other events and programs such as bible studies and Watch Night Services. Minimally, I observed worship services and neighborhoods for each congregation. However, churches for which I did not attend additional activities (for example, Watch Night events), were not in any way penalized. Instead these extra activities were considered part of a broad assessment of the goings-on for a specific church. These other types of data were considered supplementary information.

Bivariate and Regression Modeling Processes and Output

Table 1.1 (Black Church Demographics and Religious and Practical Educational Programs by Size) included demographic information and a summary of some of the religious and education programs offered by Black churches in both the Faith Factor 2000 data and the Black megachurch sample I collected. Bivariate results were presented using three categories of church size to compare and contrast church profiles in general and in light of the megachurch phenomenon. Comparisons were possible because the sample churches completed the same survey used by the PIs during the former national study. A similar process was reflected in Table 2.1 (Black Church Worship Components by Church Size). However, in that instance I compared worship features by church size. For both Tables 1.1 and 2.1, I focused on substantive rather than statistical differences because my overall goal was to present broad differences rather than highlight statistical significance, particularly because the two subsamples of Black megachurches were relatively small.

To examine possible simultaneously effects, I used the following three types of regression models based on the dependent variable under consideration; liner, logistic, and negative binomial modeling (Tables 1.2 and 4.1). In Table 1.2, whether or not Black churches offered cafeteria-style programs was examined using linear regression analysis because the dependent variable was continuous and ranged from 0 to 23 programs. In Table 4.1, I was interested in the potential effects Liberation theologies, both Black Liberation and Womanist, have on education program sponsorship. Columns 1–4 included results for four types of education-related programs using binary logistic regression analysis because the dependent variable considered two distinct 0–1 outcomes (whether or not churches sponsored tutoring, voter education, job training, and computer training). The final model presented in column 5 assessed whether churches offered the following seven types of religious education programs: bible study other than Sunday school, theological or doctrinal study, prayer and meditation groups, spiritual retreats, parenting or marriage enrichment, youth programs, and programs for young adults and singles. I employed negative binomial regression modeling because the dependent variable reflected non-negative count outcomes (Long 1997; Long and Freese 2001). In each model, the dependent variable was regressed on denomination, church and clergy demographics, and particular Black Church cultural tools. Modeling results are provided below.

Regression Model Output from Chapters 1 and 4

The following 23 religious and practical programs were included in the dependent variable *Cafeteria Programs:* food pantry/soup kitchen; cash assistance to families or individuals; thrift assistance to families or individuals; elderly, emergency, or affordable housing; counseling services or "hot line"; substance abuse programs; youth programs; tutoring or literacy programs for children and teens; voter registration or voter education; organized social issue advocacy; employment counseling, placement or training; health programs, clinics, or health education; senior citizen programs other than housing; prison or jail ministry; credit union; computer training; bible study other than Sunday school; theological or doctrinal study; prayer or meditation groups; spiritual retreats; youth religious programs; parenting or marriage enrichment; and young adults or singles' programs.

Table 1.2: Linear Regression Models of Cafeteria-Style Programs

	Model 1 Denom.	Model 2 Church Size	Model 3 Location	Model 4 Pastor	Model 5 All Variables
Baptist (1=yes)	.71 (.24)	-.01 (.25)	-.14 (.25)	-.19 (.25)	-.09 (.24)
Church Size (0-3,500+)		.01 (.01)***	.01 (.01)***	.01 (.01)***	.01 (.01)***
Urban Location (1=yes)			.81 (.27)**	.56 (.26)*	.67 (.26)**
Pastor's Profile					
Pastor's Education (None to Doctorate)				.58 (.09)***	.55 (.08)***
Pastor Is Paid (1=yes)				1.14 (.35)***	1.26 (.34)***
Church Dynamics					
Sermons: Practical Issues (5=always)					.51 (.21)*
Sermons: Spirituality (5=always)					.14 (.25)
Social Justice (5=very well)					
Assimilates New Members (5=very well)					.48 (.13)***
R^2	.01	.10	.11	.16	.24
n	1,725	1,703	1,703	1,612	1,599

Key: ***p <.001, **p <.01, *p<.05, +<.10: standard error in parenthesis. Sample weighted to reflect denominational representations. Non-Baptist is the reference group. Average Sunday Attendance: 0–3,500+. Non-Baptists include COGIC= Church of God in Christ, UM=Black United Methodist, CME=Christian Methodist Episcopal, AME=African Methodist Episcopal, Presbyterian, and AMEZ=African Methodist Episcopal Zion. Faith Factor 2000 data, N=1,863.

Table 4.1: Logistic and Negative Binomial Modeling for Black Church Education Programs

	Types of Educational Programs				
	Model 1 Tutoring	Model 2 Voter	Model 3 Employment	Model 4 Computer	Model 5 Religious
Liberation Theologies					
Black Liberation/Womanism	.21 (1.2)***	.37 (1.4)***	.19 (1.2)**	.20 (1.2)***	.01 (.01)*
Church Demographics					
Baptist (1=yes)	-.29 (.75)*	-.05 (.96)	.01 (1.0)	.01 (1.0)	.01 (.01)
Church Size (0-3,500+)	.01 (1.0)***	.01 (1.0)**	.01 (1.0)**	.01 (1.0)**	.01 (.01)***
Urban Location (1=yes)	.16 (1.2)	.03 (1.0)	.01 (1.0)	.26 (1.3)	.03 (.01)
Pastor's Profile					
Pastor's Education	.22 (1.3)***	.21 (1.2)***	.06 (1.1)	.17 (1.2)***	.01 (.01)
Pastor Is Paid (1=yes)	.08 (1.1)	.32 (1.4)	-.08 (.92)	.32 (1.4)	.03 (.02)
Church Dynamics					
Sermons: Practical Issues	.07 (1.1)	.06 (1.1)	.29 (1.3)**	-.05 (.95)	.01 (.01)
Sermons: Spirituality	.09 (1.1)	-.16 (.85)	-.01 (1.0)	.13 (1.1)	.03 (.01)
Social Justice	.11 (1.1)	.35 (1.4)***	.30 (1.4)***	.07 (1.1)	.03 (.01)***
Assimilates New Members	.11 (1.1)	.03 (1.1)	.15 (1.2)*	.18 (1.2)*	.04 (.01)***
X^2	101.0	116.4	76.8	92.8	169.6
n	1,663	1,662	1,659	1,665	1,647

Key: ***p <.001, **p <.01, *p<.05: Sample weighted to reflect denominational representations. Non-Baptist is the reference group. Pastor's education ranges from none to Doctorate. Sermons: Practical Issues (1= never, 5=always). Sermons: Spirituality (1= never, 5=always). Social Justice (1= not at all, 5=very well). Assimilates New Members (1= not at all, 5=very well). Non-Baptists include COGIC= Church of God in Christ, UM=Black United Methodist, CME=Christian Methodist Episcopal, AME=African Methodist Episcopal, Presbyterian, and AMEZ=African Methodist Episcopal Zion. Faith Factor 2000 data, N=1,863. Models 1–4 are logistic regression models and Model 5 is a negative binomial model. Odds are only provided parentheses for Models1–4 and standard errors are provided in parentheses for Model 5.

In-Depth Interview Instrument: Demographic and General Questions

1. What is your church denomination? Baptist, Church of God in Christ (COGIC), United Methodist (UM), Christian Methodist Episcopal (CME), African Methodist Episcopal (AME), African Methodist Episcopal Zion (AMEZ), Black Presbyterian.
2. What is your gender/sex? Male or female.
3. What is your age (in years)?
4. What is your official capacity at the church?
5. How would you describe the overall theology of your church? Explain.
6. How does your church determine the types of community out-

reach programs to sponsor? Explain.

7. Does church theology affect the types of community outreach programs sponsored? Explain.

8. Are you familiar with Black Liberation Theology? If so, does your church embrace this theology? Explain. What are your views about this theology?

9. Are you familiar with Womanist Theology? If so, does your church embrace this theology? Explain. What are your views about this theology?

10. Are you familiar with Prosperity theology (i.e., "health and wealth" theology)? If so, does your church embrace this theology? Explain. What are your views about this theology?

11. In the past 12 months, did your congregation provide or cooperate in providing any of the social services or community outreach programs for your own congregation's members or for people in the community? (1) Yes (2) No.

a. Food pantry or soup kitchen, b. Cash assistance to families or individuals, c. Thrift store or thrift store donations, d. Elderly, emergency, or affordable housing, e. Counseling services or "hot lines," f. Substance abuse programs, g. Youth programs, h. Tutoring or literacy programs for children and teens, i. Voter registration or voter education, j. Organized social issue advocacy, k. Employment counseling, placement, or training, l. Health programs, clinics, or health education, m. Senior citizen programs other than housing, n. Prison or jail ministry, o. Credit unions, p. Computer training, q. HIV/AIDS ministry, r. Other.

12. Now, for each one, please say whether you (4) strongly approve, (3) somewhat approve, (2) somewhat disapprove, or (1) strongly disapprove:

a. Clergy in your own church taking part in protest marches on civil rights issues.

b. Churches expressing their views on day-to-day social and political issues.

c. Churches taking part in activities to combat poverty.

d. Churches taking part in activities to combat HIV/AIDS.

e. A woman as pastor of a church.

f. Churches taking part in activities to combat racism.

g. Churches taking part in activities to combat sexism.

13. Is your church involved in community outreach activities or programs specifically to address HIV/AIDS? If so, describe them? How long has your church been involved in these activities? Why did your church become involved in these activities?

14. Is your church involved in community outreach activities or programs specifically to address poverty? If so, describe them? How long has your church been involved in these activities? Why did your church become involved in these activities?

15. Should the Black Church be involved in programs to combat HIV/AIDS? Explain.

16. Should the Black Church be involved in programs to combat poverty? Explain.

Church Profile Survey

(Certain data for latter source were collected through church historical material, websites, and pastoral and church leader interviews.)

A. Congregational Climate:
How well does each of the following statements describe your congregation? Using a scale from 1 to 5 where "5" describes your congregation very well, and "1" means not at all well.
a. Your congregation is spiritually vital and "alive" _____
b. Your congregation is working for social justice _____
c. Your congregation helps members deepen their relationship with God _____
d. Your congregation gives strong expression to its denomination heritage _____
e. Members are excited about the future of your congregation _____
f. New people are easily assimilated into the life of your congregation _____

B. What is the total attendance for all services on a typical Sunday? _____

C. Sermonic Focus:
How often does the sermon focus on the following subjects? Would you say (5) always, (4) often, (3) sometimes, (2) seldom, or (1) never?
a. Practical advice for daily living _____
b. References to the racial situation in society _____
c. References to Black Liberation theology _____
d. References to Womanist theology _____
e. References to Prosperity theology _____

D. In your Sunday school, what is the typical, total weekly attendance?
Adults: _____ Children: _____

E. Church Dynamics:
a. Thinking about the ministerial and program staff, how many does this congregation have? _____, full-time paid staff _____, and part-time paid staff _____
b. Just your best estimate, what is the number of persons on the membership roll of this congregation? _____
c. Of the total number of regularly participating adults, what total percent would you estimate are the following: college graduates _____, ages 18-35 years old _____, from household incomes below $20,000 _____.
d. How would you describe your congregation's financial health? Good, tight, or in serious difficulty.

Faith Factor 2000 Project Data

The data are a national secondary database of Black churches based on a joint venture between the Interdenominational Theological Center (ITC) in Atlanta, Georgia and the Lilly Foundation to provide a profile of such churches in the United States. Data collection was spearheaded by the ITC with assistance from Gallup, Inc. The file includes 1,863 Black churches from the following five African American denominations; Baptist [502 churches], Church of God in Christ (COGIC) [503], Christian

Methodist Episcopal (CME) [295], African Methodist Episcopal (AME) [257], and African Methodist Episcopal Zion (AMEZ) [110]. Predominately Black churches from the historically White United Methodist and Presbyterian denominations—United Methodist (UM) [95] and Black Presbyterian [101]—were also included for a total of seven denominations. The sampling frame and sample selection took place in several phases. First, lists of all the churches in the AME, AMEZ, CME, COGIC, UM, and Presbyterian denominations were provided by denominational heads or deans from the various schools at the ITC. The decentralized nature of the Baptist polity prevented such a list. To develop the Baptist sampling frame, ITC solicited information from Tri-Media, an organization that retains lists of all churches nationwide that purchase Sunday school material and supplies. Tri-Media data were used to identify the population of Baptist churches affiliated with the three largest historically African American Baptist denominations. Although the sampling frame for Baptist churches is an approximation with several clear limitations, it represents a systematic attempt to identify such congregations given their lack of national hierarchy. After the seven lists were compiled, Gallup selected a random sample from each denomination to meet the desired subsample sizes. Gallup conducted telephone surveys of clergy and senior lay leaders February 22, 2000, through May 11, 2000. Each interview averaged about 16 minutes in length and 37 questions were asked. The church leaders were required to provide aggregate demographic church data as well as answer attitudinal and behavioral questions on topics such as church financial health, spirituality, worship and identity, missions, leadership and organizational dynamics, church climate, and community involvement. Initial screening was used to gain cooperation from the pastor and to confirm denomination. If the pastor was unavailable, an assistant pastor or senior lay leader was interviewed. Of the 1,863 interviews, 77 percent (1,482) were conducted with pastors and 23 percent (381) were conducted with an assistant pastor or senior lay leader. Senior clergy was used because they are expected to be most knowledgeable about their respective congregations. Refer to Barnes (2004) for additional information about the data collection process. [note: Q=Question]

Variable Operationalizations for Quantitative Analyses

1. Sunday Attendance (continuous, 0–6,000): Q: What is the total attendance for all services on a typical Sunday?

Denomination

2. Denomination (coded into seven 0–1 dummy variables, Baptist is the reference category): Q: What is your church denomination? Baptist, Church of God in Christ (COGIC), United Methodist (UM), Christian Methodist Episcopal (CME), African Methodist Episcopal (AME), African Methodist Episcopal Zion (AMEZ), Presbyterian (P).

Demographics

3. Urban (1=yes) (Gallup determined the state and region for each church and the final category).
4. Paid pastor (coded 0=volunteer, 1=paid): Q: Are you/is your pastor paid or a volunteer?
5. What is the highest level of (your/your pastor's) ministerial education? None, apprenticeship with senior pastor, certificate or correspondence program, bible college or some seminary, seminary degree (for example, Minister of Divinity), post-Minister of Divinity work or degree (for example, D. Min)?

Church Worship and Teaching

6. Sermons Q: How well does each of the following statements describe the sermon focus? (a) Practical advice, (b) Personal spiritual growth, (c) Black Liberation theology or Womanist theology. Use a scale from 1 to 5 where "5" means always and "1" means never.
7. Worship Music Q: During your congregation's regular worship services, how often are the following included as part of the service? (a) spirituals, (b) gospel music, (c) gospel rap music, (d) dance or drama. Use a scale from 1 to 5 where "5" means always and "1" means never.

8. Worship and Teaching Q: How important are the following in the worship and teaching of your congregation? (a) sacred scripture, (b) historical creeds, (c) presence of Holy Spirit, (d) personal experience. Use a scale from 1 to 4 where "1" means little or no importance and "4" means extremely important.

Programs

9. Religious Programs Q: During the past 12 months, did your congregation participate in any of the following programs or activities in addition to your regular Sunday school? Bible study other than Sunday school, theological or doctrinal study, prayer or mediation groups, or spiritual retreats.

10. Social and Community Outreach Programs Q: In the past 12 months, did your congregation provide or cooperate in providing for any of these social services or community outreach programs?" Food pantry, cash assistance, thrift store, elder housing or affordable housing, counseling/hot lines, substance abuse, youth programs, tutoring/literary programs for youth and teens, voter registration or voter education, social issue advocacy, employment counseling/placement or training, health programs/clinics or health education, senior citizens programs other than housing, prison or jail ministry, credit unions, and computer training.

Social Activism

11. Social Justice Q: How well does each of the following statements describe your congregation's focus? Working for social justice. Use a scale from 1 to 5 where "5" describes your congregation very well and "1" means not at all well.

New Members

12. Assimilation Q: How well does each of the following statements describe your congregation's focus? New people are easily assimilated into the life of your congregation. Use a scale from 1 to 5 where "5" describes your congregation very well and "1" means not at all well.

Black Megachurch Sample:
Church Survey Summary

This book focused on 16 Black megachurches. This section provides an overview of their demographic composition. Regarding location, 56 percent (9) of the churches are part of urban areas, 37.5 percent (6) are suburban, and one (6.25 percent) is a rural church. Church size ranges from approximately 1,375 persons each Sunday to well over 25,000. The average membership size is 8,039 persons. About 75 percent (12) of the congregations can be considered class diverse. Two churches have memberships that are predominately middle- and upper-class, while two of them have memberships that are predominately working class or poor. All pastors are full-time clergy and 13 (81 percent) have earned at least a Doctor of Ministry degree. Five of the pastors are or have been officially involved in politics (2 senators, 1 past congressman, 1 long-time delegate, and 1 super-delegate). All of the churches sponsor religious, poverty, and community service programs. About 11 churches (69 percent) offer in-house HIV/AIDS programs; most are comprehensive in nature. Thirteen (13 or 81 percent) have CDCs; 10 churches (62.5 percent) have or currently receive faith-based funding. On average, 75 percent (12) of the congregations sponsor 40 or more programs/ministries.

References

Ainsworth-Darnell, James and Douglas Downey. 1998. "Assessing the Oppositional Culture Explanation for Racial/Ethnic Differences in School Performance." *American Sociological Review* 63: 536–53.

Aivaz, Mike and Adam Doster. 2008. "Televangelist Spreads the 'Gospel of Bling,' Lands Himself in Hot Water." (January 18, 2008). Retrieved April 24, 2008 from http://rawstory.com/news/2007/Nightline_The_Gospel_of_bling_0118.html.

Allen, Richard. 1960. *The Life, Experience, and Gospel Labors of the Rt. Rev. Richard Allen.* Edited by G. Singleton. Nashville, TN: Abingdon Press.

Allport, Gordon W. 1966. "Religious Context of Prejudice." *Journal for the Scientific Study of Religion* 5: 447–57.

Anderson, Elijah and Jerry Van Hoy. 2006. "Striving for Self-Sufficient Families: Urban and Rural Experiences for Women in Welfare-to-Work Programs." *Journal of Poverty: Innovations on Social, Political & Economic Inequalities* 10(1): 69–91.

Anthony, Michael. 2001. *Introducing Christian Education: Foundations for the Twenty-first Century.* Grand Rapids, MI: Baker Academic.

Archbald, Douglas. 2004. "School Choice, Magnet Schools, and the Liberation Model: An Empirical Study." *Sociology of Education* 77(4): 283–310.

Babbie, Earl. 2002. *The Basics of Social Research* (2nd ed.). Belmont, CA: Wadsworth/Thomson Learning.

Ballard, Scotty and Javonne Stewart. 2006. "The Ministry of Hip Hop." *Jet* 110(8): 30–3.

Banks, James. 2001. *Cultural Diversity and Education: Foundations, Curriculum and Teaching* (4th ed.). Boston: Allyn & Bacon.

Barnes, Sandra. 2009. "Religion and Rap Music: An Analysis of Black Church Usage." *Review of Religious Research* 49(3): 319–38.

_____. 2007. "Structure vs. Agency: A Case Study of the Experiences of the Working Poor." *Journal of Poverty* 12(2): 175–200.

———. 2006. "Whosoever Will Let *Her* Come: Gender Inclusivity in the Black Church." *Journal for the Scientific Study of Religion* 45(3): 371–87.

———. 2005. "Black Church Culture and Community Action." *Social Forces.* 84(2): 967–94.

_____. 2005b. *The Cost of Being Poor: A Comparative Study of Life in Poor Urban Neighborhoods in Gary, Indiana.* New York: State University Press of New York.

———. 2005c. "Too Poor to Get Sick? The Implications of Place, Race, and Costs on the Health Care Experiences of Residents in Poor Urban Neighborhoods." *Research in the Sociology of Health Care* 22: 47–64.

———. 2004. "Priestly and Prophetic Influences on Black Church Social Services." *Social Problems* 51(2): 202–21.

Barnes, Sandra and Charles Jaret. 2003. "The 'American Dream' in Poor Urban Neighborhoods: An Analysis of Home Ownership Attitudes and Behavior and Financial Saving Behavior." *Sociological Focus* 36(3): 219–39.

Battle, Michael. 2006. *The Black Church in America: African American Christian Spirituality.* Malden, MA: Blackwell Publishing.

Bellah, Robert, Richard Madsen, William M. Sullivan, Ann Swidler, and Steven Tipton. 1996. *Habits of the Heart: Individualism and Commitment in American Life.* Berkeley: University of California Press.

Benford, Robert D. 1993."'You Could Be the Hundredth Monkey': Collective Action Frames and Vocabularies of Motive within the Nuclear Disarmament Movement." *The Sociological Quarterly* 34(2): 195–216.

Bickman, Leonard and Debra Rog (eds.). 1998. *Handbook of Applied Social Research Methods.* Thousand Oaks, CA: Sage Publications.

Billingsley, Andrew. 1999. *Mighty Like a River: The Black Church and Social Reform.* New York: Oxford University Press.

———.1992. *Climbing Jacob's Ladder: The Enduring Legacy of African-American Families.* New York: A Touchstone Book.

Blumer, Herbert. 1958. Race Prejudice as a Sense of Group Position. *Pacific Sociological Review* 1(1): 3–7.

Bonilla-Silva, Eduardo. 2006. *Racism without Racists: Color-Blind Racism and the Persistence of Racial Inequality in the United States.* Lanham, MD: Rowman & Littlefield Publishers, Inc.

Bourdieu, Pierre. 1984. *Distinction: A Social Critique of the Judgment of Taste.* Cambridge, MA: Harvard University Press.

———.1977. *Outline of a Theory of Practice.* Cambridge, England: Cambridge University Press.

Brown, Tony N., David R. Williams, James S. Jackson, Harold W. Neighbors, Myriam Torres, Sherrill L. Sellers, and Kendrick T. Brown. 1999. "Being Black and Feeling Blue: The Mental Health Consequences of Racial Discrimination." *Race and Society* 2(2): 117–31.

Bryk, Anthony, Valerie Lee, and Peter Holland. 1993. *Catholic Schools and the Common Good*. Cambridge, MA: Harvard University Press.

Bureau of Justice Statistics. 1999. *1998 BJS Sourcebook*. Bureau of Justice Statistics, U.S. Department of Justice: (August).

Calhoun-Brown, Allison. 1999. "The Image of God: Black Theology and Racial Empowerment in the African American Community." *Review of Religious Research* 40(3): 197–211.

Cannon, Katie. 1988. *Black Womanist Ethics*. Atlanta, GA: Scholars Press.

Carter, Harold A.1976. *The Prayer Tradition of Black People*. Valley Forge, PA: Judson Press.

Center for Educational Reform. 2001. *National Charter School Directory*. Retrieved January 5, 2008 at http://www.edreform.com/Press_Box/Press_Release/index.cfm

Centers for Disease Control and Prevention. 2008. Behavioral Risk Factor Surveillance System Data. Retrieved July 13, 2009 from http://www.statehealthfacts.org/comparebar.jsp?ind=91&cat=2.

———. 2004. *HIV/AIDS Surveillance Report, 14*. Atlanta: U.S. Department of Health and Human Services.

———. 2003. *Division of HIV/AIDS Annual Report, 2002*. Atlanta: U.S. Department of Health and Human Services.

———. 2002. "Drug-Associated HIV Transmission Continues in the United States." (May). Rockville, Maryland.

Chaves. 2004. *Congregations in America*. Cambridge, MA: Harvard University Press.

Clark, M.L. 1991. "Social Identity, Peer Relations, and Academic Competence of African American Adolescents." *Education and Urban Society* 24(1): 14–26.

Coleman, James and Thomas Hoffer. 1987. *Public and Private High School: The Impact of Communities*. New York: Basic Books.

Collins, Patricia Hill. 2009. *Another Kind of Public Education: Race, Schools, the Media and Democratic Possibilities*. Boston, MA: Beacon Press.

———. 2004. *Black Sexual Politics: African Americans, Gender, and the New Racism*. New York: Routledge.

_____. 2000. *Black Feminist Thought: Knowledge, Consciousness, and the Politics of Empowerment*. New York: Routledge.

Cone, James. 2004. "Calling the Oppressors to Account: God and Black Suffering." Pp. 3–12 in *Living Stones in the Household of God: The Legacy and Future of Black Theology*, edited by Linda Thomas. Minneapolis, MN: Fortress Press.

_____. 1997. *God of the Oppressed*. Maryknoll, NY: Orbis Books.

_____. 1995. "Black Theology as Liberation Theology." Pp. 177–207 in *African American*

Religious Studies: An Interdisciplinary Anthology, edited by Gayraud Wilmore. Durham, NC: Duke University Press.

_____. 1972. *The Spirituals and the Blues*. Maryknoll, NY: Orbis Books.

_____. 1969[1999]. *Black Theology and Black Power*. Maryknoll, New York: Orbis Books.

Costen, Melva Wilson. 1995. "Singing Praise to God in African American Worship Contexts." Pp. 392–404 in *African American Religious Studies: An Interdisciplinary Anthology*, edited by Gayraud Wilmore. Durham, NC: Duke University Press.

_____. 1993. *African-American Christian Worship*. Nashville, TN: Abingdon Press.

Dart, John. 1991. "Themes of Bigness, Success Attract Independent Churches Ministry." *Los Angeles Times* (July 20): 14.

Davis, Donna. 2004. "Merry-Go-Round: A Return to Segregation and the Implications for Creating Democratic Schools." *Urban Education* 39(4): 394–407.

Davis, Herndon L. 2005. "God, Gays, and the Black Church: Keeping the Faith within the Black Community." *AOL Black Voices*, Sept, 1, from http://blackvoices.aol.com/black_liefstyle/soutl_spirit_headlines_features/canvas/feature.

Dee, Thomas and Helen Fu. 2004. "Do Charter Schools Skim Students or Drain Resources." *Economics of Education Review* 23: 259–71.

Dempsey, V. and G. Nobilt. 1996. "Cultural Ignorance and School Desegregation." Pp. 119–37 in *Beyond Desegregation: The Politics of Quality in African American Schooling*, edited by M.J. Shujaa. Thousand Oaks, CA: Corwin Press.

Denzin, Norman and Yvonna Lincoln. 2005. *The Sage Handbook of Qualitative Research*. Thousand Oaks, CA: Sage.

Drake, St. Clair. 1940. *Churches and Voluntary Associations in the Chicago Negro Community*. Chicago, IL: Works Projects Administration District 3.

Drake, St. Clair and Horace R. Cayton. 1985. "The Churches of Bronzeville." Pp. 349–63 in *Afro-American Religious History: A Documentary Witness*, edited by Milton C. Sernett. Durham, NC: Duke University Press.

_____.1942[1962]. *Black Metropolis: A Study of Negro Life in a Northern City Vol. I and II*. New York: Harper and Row.

DuBois, W.E.B. 1903[2003]. *The Negro Church*. Walnut Creek, CA: Altimira Press.

Durkheim, Emile. 1964. *The Division of Labor in Society*. New York: Free Press.

Dyson, Michael. 1996. *Race Rules: Navigating the Color Line*. New York: Vintage Books.

Eakle, A. Jonathan. 2007. "Literacy Spaces of a Christian Faith-Based School." *Reading Research Quarterly* 42(4): 472–510.

Edin, Katherine and L. Lein. 1996. "Work, Welfare, and Single Mothers' Economic Survival Strategies." *American Sociological Review* 61: 253–66.

Edwards, Korie. 2009. "Race, Religion, and Worship: Are Contemporary African-American Worship Practices Distinct?" *Journal for the Scientific Study of Religion* 48(1): 30–52.

Ehrlich, Dimitri. 1997. "Keeping the Faith: Interview with K. Franklin." *Interview*. 27(9): 144–6.

Ellingson, Stephen. 2007. *The Megachurch and the Mainline: Remaking Religious Tradition in the Twenty-First Century*. Chicago, IL: University of Chicago Press.

Ellison, Christoper and Darren Sherkat. 1995. "The 'Semi-Involuntary Institution' Revisited: Regional Variations in Church Participation among Black Americans." *Social Forces* 73(4): 1415–437.

Feagin, Joe. 2006. *Systemic Racism: A Theory of Oppression*. New York: Routledge.

Felder, Cain Hope (ed.).1991. *Stony the Road We Trod: African American Biblical Interpretation*. Minneapolis, MN: Fortress Press.

Fellmeth, Robert. 2005. "Child Poverty in the United States." *Human Rights: Journal of the Section of Individual Rights & Responsibilities* 32(1): 2–19.

A First Look at the Literacy of America's Adults in the 21st Century. Retrieved April 15, 2008 from http://nces.ed.gov/ssbr/pages/adultliteracy.asp?IndID=32.

Fiske, Edward and Helen Ladd. 2000. *When Schools Compete: A Cautionary Tale*. Washington, D.C.: Brookings Institution Press.

Floyd-Thomas, Stacey. 2006. *Mining the Motherlode: Methods in Womanist Ethics*. Cleveland, OH: The Pilgrim Press.

Fountain, John. 2005. "No Place for Me: I Still Love God, but I've Lost Faith in the Black Church." *Washington Post* (July 17): B01.

Franklin, V.P., Lynn Gordon, Maxine Schwartz, and Paula Fass. 1991. "Understanding American Education in the Twentieth Century." *History of Education Quarterly* 31(1): 47–65.

Frazier, Edward Franklin. 1964. *The Negro Church in America*. New York: Schocken Books.

Fulton, Delawese. 2007. "Education of a Generation: Program Gives Young Adults an Up-Close Look at Business, Government." *South Carolina Press Clipping Bureau* (April 19): 7B–8B.

Gabbidon, Shaun and Steven Peterson. 2006. "Living While Black: A State-Level Analysis of the Influence of Select Social Stressors on the Quality of Life among Black Americans." *Journal of Black Studies* 37(1): 83–102.

Gallagher, Charles. 2008. *Rethinking the Color Line: Readings in Race and Ethnicity* (4th ed.). New York: McGraw-Hill.

Gallup, George and Jim Castelli. 1989. *The People's Religion: American Faith in the 90's*. New York: Macmillan.

Garibaldi, Antoine (ed.). 1984. *Black Colleges and Universities: Challenges for the Future*. New York: Praeger.

Giddings, Paula. 1984. *When and Where I Enter: The Impact of Black Women on Race and Sex in America*. New York: William Morrow.

Gilbreath, Edward. 1994. "The Birth of a Megachurch." *Christianity Today* 38(8): 23.

Gilkes, Cheryl Townsend. 2001. *If It Wasn't for the Women: Black Women's Experience and Womanist Culture in Church and Community*. New York: Orbis Books.

Goffman, Irving. 1974. *Frame Analysis*. Boston, MA: Northeastern University Press.

Graham, Jeana. 2009. "HBCU's Economic Struggle Prompts Calls for Merging."

Retrieved August 21, 2009. from http://www.ncc.com/2009/LIVING/wayof
life/05/18/what.matters. black.universities/index.html.

Grant, Jacquelyn. 1989. *White Women's Christ and Black Women's Jesus: Feminist Christology and Womanist Response.* Atlanta, GA: Scholars Press.

Hall, Stuart. 1983. "What Is the 'Black' in Black Popular Culture?" Pp. 21–33 in *Black Popular Culture*, edited by Gina Dent. New York: The New Press.

Hallinan, Maureen. 2001. "Sociological Perspectives on Black–White Inequalities in American Schooling." *Sociology of Education* 74: 50–70.

Harrison, Milmon. 2005. *Righteous Riches.* New York: Oxford University Press.

Harrison, P.M. and Beck, A.J. 2006. *Prison and Jail Inmates at Midyear 2005.* Washington, DC: US Dept. of Justice, Office of Justice Programs, Bureau of Justice Statistics.

Hartford Institute of Religious Research. 2005. Mega Churches Today: Summary of Data from the Faith Communities Today Project, 1–16.

Haynes, Lemuel. 1985. "A Black Puritan's Farewell." Pp. 51–59 in *Afro-American Religious History: A Documentary Witness*, edited by Milton C. Sernett. Durham, NC: Duke University Press.

Higginbotham, Evelyn Brooks. 1993. *Righteous Discontent: The Women's Movement in the Black Baptist Church 1880–1920.* Cambridge, MA: Harvard University Press.

Hill, Kenneth H. H. 2007. *Religious Education in the African American Tradition.* Atlanta, GA: Chalice Press.

Hodgson, Peter and Robert King (eds.).1994. *Christian Theology: An Introduction to Its' Traditions and Tasks.* Minneapolis, MN: Fortress Press.

The Holy Bible: New Revised Standard Version. 1989. Nashville, TN: Thomas Nelson.

Jarrett, Robin. 1994. "Living Poor: Family Life among Single Parent, African-American Women." *Social Problems* 41(1): 30–49.

Johnson, Deborah. 2000. "Disentangling Poverty and Race." *Applied Developmental Science* (Supplement) 4:55–68.

The Journal of Blacks in Higher Education. 2008. "Black Student College Graduation Rates Inch Higher but a Large Racial Gap Persists." Retrieved March 15, 2008 from http://www.jbhe.com/preview/winter07preview.html.

The Journal of Blacks in Higher Education. 2000–1."African-American Parents Should Not Dismiss the Value of Charter Schools in Preparing Their Children for College." 30 (Winter): 72–4.

King, Jason L. 2004. *On the Down Low: A Journey into the Lives of "Straight" Black Men Who Sleep with Men.* New York: Broadway Books.

King, Robert. 1994. "Introduction: The Task of Theology." Pp. 1–34 in *Christian Theology: An Introduction to Its Traditions and Tasks*, edited by Peter Hodgson and Robert King. Minneapolis: Fortress Press.

Kopano, Baruti. 2002. "Rap Music as an Extension of the Black Rhetorical Tradition: 'Keepin' It Real.'" *The Western Journal of Black Studies* 26(4): 204–13.

Krippendorf, Klaus. 1980. *Content Analysis: An Introduction to Its Methodology.* Beverly

Hills, CA: Sage Publications.

Lacireno-Paquet, Natalie, Thomas Holyoke, Michele Moser, and Jeffrey Henig. 2002. "Creaming Versus Cropping: Charter School Enrollment Practices in Response to Market Incentives." *Educational Evaluation and Policy Analysis* 24(2): 145–58.

LeBlanc, Douglas. 2001. "T-Bone: The Last Street Preacha." *Christianity Today* 45(6): 111.

Lee, Shayne. 2007. "Prosperity Theology: T.D. Jakes and the Gospel of the Almighty Dollar." *Cross Currents* 58(2): 227–37.

———2005. *T.D. Jakes: America's New Preacher.* New York: New York University Press.

Lincoln, C. Eric. 1984. *Race, Religion and the Continuing American Dilemma.* New York: Hill and Wang.

Lincoln, C. Eric and Lawrence H. Mamiya. 1990. *The Black Church in the African— American Experience.* Durham, NC: Duke University Press.

Long, J.S. 1997. *Regression Models for Categorical and Limited Dependent Variables.* Thousand Oaks, CA: Sage.

Long, J.S. and Freese, J. 2001. *Regression Models for Categorical Dependent Variables Using Stata.* College Station, TX: Stata Press.

Lykens, Kristine and Paul Jargowsky. 2002. "Medicaid Matters: Children's Health and Medicaid Eligibility Expansions." *Journal of Policy Analysis and Management* 21(2): 219–38.

Lynn, Marvin et al. 1999. "Raising the Critical Consciousness of African American Students in Baldwin Hills: A Portrait of an Exemplary African American Male Teacher." *The Journal of Negro Education* 68(1): 42–53.

MacMaster, Samuel A., Jenny L. Jones, Randolph F.R. Rasch, Sharon L. Crawford, Stephanie Thompson, and Edwin C. Sanders, II. 2007. "Evaluation of a Faith-Based Culturally Relevant Program for African American Substance Users at Risk for HIV in the Southern United States." *Research on Social Work Practice* 17(2): 229–38.

Matthews-Armstead, Eunice. 2002. "And Still They Rise: College Enrollment of African American Women from Poor Communities." *Journal of Black Studies* 33(1): 44–65.

Mays, Benjamin and Joseph Nicholson. 1933. *The Negro's Church.* New York: Institute of Social and Religious Research.

McRoberts, Omar M. 2003. *Streets of Glory: Church and Community in a Black Urban Neighborhood.* Chicago, IL: University of Chicago Press.

———.1999. "Understanding the 'New' Black Pentecostal Activism: Lessons from Ecumenical Urban Ministries in Boston." *Sociology of Religion* 60(1): 47–70.

Mills, Charles Wright. 1956. *The Power Elite.* New York: Oxford University Press.

Mitchem, Stephanie Y. 2002. *Introducing Womanist Theology.* New York: Orbis Books.

Montecel, Maria, Josie Cortez, and Albert Cortez. 2004. "Dropout-Prevention Programs: Right Intent, Wrong Focus, and Some Suggestions on Where To God from Here." *Education and Urban Society* 36(2): 169–88.

Morris, Aldon D. 1984. *The Origins of the Civil Rights Movement: Black Communities Organizing for Change.* New York: The Free Press.

Morris, Jerome. 2004. "Can Anything Good Come from Nazareth? Race, Class, and African American Schooling and Community in the Urban South and Midwest." *American Educational Research Journal* 41(1): 69–112.

Morthland, John. 1997. "Heavenly: K. Franklin and God's Property." *Texas Monthly* 25: 28.

Mosby-Avery, Karen. 2004. "Black Theology and the Black Church." Pp. 33–36 in *Living Stones in the Household of God: The Legacy and Future of Black Theology*, edited by Linda Thomas. Minneapolis, MN: Fortress Press.

Mossberger, Karen, Caroline J. Tolbert, and Mary Stansbury. 2003. *Virtual Inequality: Beyond the Digital Divide*. Washington, D.C.: Georgetown University Press.

National Center for Child Poverty. 2002. *Child Poverty Fact Sheet: March 2002*. Columbia University. http://cpmcnet.columbia.edu/dept/nccp/ycpf.html.

Nelsen, Hart M. and Anne K. Nelsen. 1975. *The Black Church in the Sixties*. Lexington: University of Kentucky Press.

Nettles, S.M. 1991. "Community Contributions to School Outcomes of African American Students." *Education and Urban Society* 24(1): 73–86.

Neuman, Susan. 2002. *Oh, God! A Black Woman's Guide to Sex and Spirituality*. Toronto, Canada: One World/Ballantine Books.

Niebuhr, Gustav. 1995. "Megachurches: The Gospels of Management." *The New York Times* (April 18): Section A, Column 1: 1–4.

———. 1995a. "Where Religion Gets a Big Dose of Shopping-Mall Culture." *The New York Times* (April 16): Section 1, Column 1: 1–3.

Norris, Pippa. 2001. *Digital Divide: Civic Engagement, Information Poverty, and the Internet Worldwide*. New York: Cambridge University Press.

Nowak, Jeremy. 2001. "Community Development and Religious Institutions." Pp. 111–126 in *Sacred Places, Civic Purposes: Should Government Help Faith-Based Charity?*, edited by E.J. Dionne Jr. and Ming Hsu Chen. Washington, D.C.: Boston University Press.

Ogbu, John. 1991. "Low Performance as an Adaptation: The Case of Black in Stockton, California." Pp. 249–85 in *Minority Status and Schooling*, edited by M.A. Gibson and J. Ogbu. New York: Grand Publishing.

———. 1978. *Minority Education and Caste*. New York: Academic Press.

Oliver, Cedric. 2005. *Spiritual Storms: Conquest Over Crisis*. Gary, IN: Reap Publications.

Omi, Michael and Howard Winant. 1994. *Racial Formation in the United States: From the 1960s to the 1990s*. New York: Routledge.

Ostling, R.N. and Minal Hajratwala. 1991. "Superchurhces and How They Grow." *Time* 138(5): 62–3.

Owens, Susie. 2003. *Memorable Moments*. Washington, DC.

Pattillo, Mary. 2007. *Black on the Block: The Politics of Race and Class in the City*. Chicago, IL: University of Chicago Press.

Pattillo-McCoy, Mary. 1999. *Black Picket Fences: Privilege and Peril among the Black Middle Class*. Chicago, IL: University of Chicago Press.

———. 1998."Church Culture as a Strategy of Action in the Black Community." *American Sociological Review* 63: 767–84.

Peck, Laura R. and Elizabeth A. Segal. 2006. "The Latent and Sequential Costs of Being Poor: Exploration of a Potential Paradigm Shift." *Journal of Poverty: Innovations on Social, Political & Economic Inequalities* 10(1): 1–24.

Potter, Cathryn C. and Susan Klein-Rothschild. 2002. "Getting Home on Time: Predicting Timely Permanence for Young Children." *Child Welfare* 81(2): 123–50.

Ravitch, Diane. 2000. *Left Back: A Century of Battles Over School Reform*. New York: Simon & Schuster.

Research Policy Practice International. 2000. *The State of Charter Schools 2000*. Washington, D.C.: U.S. Department of Education, Office of Educational Research and Improvement.

Rivera, John. 2002. "Neo-Pentecostals: Traditional Congregations Bristle at Stress on the Individual over Social Activism." *The Baltimore Sun.* Aug. 25, 2002. http://sunspot.net/.

Rodenborg, Nancy. 2004. "Services to African American Children in Poverty: Institutional Discrimination in Child Welfare?" *Journal of Poverty* 8(3): 109–30.

Rupon, Kristy E. 2007. "Atlas Road Project to Launch Sunday." *South Carolina Press Clipping Bureau* (April 21): A1, A9.

Schaller, Lyle. 2000. *The Very Large Church*. Nashville, TN: Abingdon Press.

———.1990. "Megachurch!" *Christianity Today* 34(4): 20–4.

Sernett, Milton (ed.). 1985. *Afro-American Religious History: A Documentary Witness*. Durham, NC: Duke University Press.

Seymour, Jack L. 1997. *Mapping Christian Education: Approaches to Congregational Learning*. Nashville, TN: Abingdon Press.

Shapiro, Thomas. 2004. *The Hidden Cost of Being African American: How Wealth Perpetuates Inequality*. New York: Oxford University Press.

Sherkat, Darren and Christopher Ellison. 1991."The Politics of Black Religious Change: Disaffiliation from Black Mainline Denominations." *Social Forces* 70(2): 431–54.

Shipler, David K. 2004. *The Working Poor: Invisible in America*. New York: Alfred A. Knopf.

Siddle-Walker, E.V. 1996. "Can Institutions Care? Evidence from the Segregated Schooling of African American Children." Pp. 211–26 in *Beyond Desegregation: The Politics of Quality in African American Schooling*, edited by M.J. Shujaa. Thousand Oaks, CA: Corwin Press.

Simmons, Joseph, Daryl McDaniels, and Amy Linden. 1993. "Niggas with Beatitude." *Transition*. 62: 176–87.

Smith Sr., J. Alfred and Jini Kilgore (eds.) 2006. *Speak until Justice Wakes: Prophetic Reflections from J. Alfred Smith Sr*. Valley Forge, PA: Judson Press.

Stack, Carol. 1974. *All Our Kin: Strategies for Survival in a Black Community*. New York: Harper and Row.

Swidler, Ann. 1995. "Cultural Power and Social Movements." Pp. 25–40 in *Social Movements and Culture*, Vol. 4, *Social Movements, Protest, and Contention*, edited by H. Johnston and B. Klandermans. Minneapolis: University of Minnesota Press.

———.1986. "Culture in Action: Symbols and Strategies." *American Sociological Review* 51: 273–86.

Talbert, Marcia W. 2009. "HBCU Students Seek More Avenues for Funding." *Black Enterprise* (April 23). Retrieved August 31, 2009. http://www.blackenterprise.com-/wealth-for-life/2009/04/23/hbcu-students-seek-more-avenues-for-funding.

Taylor, Robert. 1988. "Correlates of Religious Non-Involvement among Black Americans." *Review of Religious Research* 30: 126–39.

Thomas, Linda. 2004. "Introduction." Pp. x–xiv in *Living Stones in the Household of God: The Legacy and Future of Black Theology*, edited by Linda Thomas. Minneapolis, MN: Fortress Press.

———. 2004a. "Womanist Theology, Epistemology, and a New Anthropological Paradigm." Pp. 37–48 in *Living Stones in the Household of God: The Legacy and Future of Black Theology*, edited by Linda Thomas. Minneapolis, MN: Fortress Press.

———.1998. "Womanist Theology, Epistemology, and a New Anthropological Paradigm." *Cross Currents* 48(4): 1–14.

Thompson, Sr., Leroy. 1999. *Money Thou Art Loosed!* Darrow, LA: Ever Increasing Word Ministries.

Thumma, Scott. 1996. "Megachurches of Atlanta." Pp. 199–213 in *Religions of Atlanta: Religious Diversity in the Centennial Olympic City*, edited by Gary Laderman. Atlanta, GA: Scholars Press.

Thumma, Scott and Dave Travis. 2007. *Beyond Megachurch Myths: What We Can Learn from America's Largest Churches*. San Francisco: John Wiley & Sons.

Townes, Emilie. 2006. *Womanist Ethnics and the Cultural Production of Evil*. New York: Palgrave Macmillan.

Tucker, Tamelyn. 2002. "Bringing the Church 'Back In'": Black Megachurches and Community Development Activities." Dissertation.

Tucker-Worgs, Tamelyn. 2002. "Get on Board, Little Children, There's Room for Many More: The Black Mega Church Phenomenon." *The Journal of the Interdenominational Theological Center* XXIX (1–2): 177–203.

U.S. Bureau of the Census. 2007. "Census Current Population Survey Annual Social and Economic Supplement." Washington, D.C.: U.S. Government Printing Office. http://www.census.gov.

Vaugh, John. 1993. *Megachurches & America's Cities: How Churches Grow*. Grand Rapids, MI: Baker Books.

Wang, Youfa and May A. Beydoun. 2007. "The Obesity Epidemic in the United States— Gender, Age, Socioeconomic, Racial/Ethnic and Geographic Characteristics: A

Systematic Review and Meta-Regression Analysis." Johns Hopkins Bloomberg School of Public Health. Retrieved July 13, 2007 from http://www.jhsph.edu/publichealthnews/press_releases/2007/wang_adult_obesity.html.

Weber, Max. 1946. *From Max Weber: Essays in Sociology*. New York: Oxford University Press.

———.1930. *The Protestant Ethic and the Spirit of Capitalism*. Los Angeles: Roxbury Publishing.

Weems, Renita. 2002. *Showing Mary: How Women Can Share Prayers, Wisdom, and the Blessings of God*. West Bloomfield, MI: Warner Books.

Wells, Amy et al. 2000. "Charter Schools and Racial and Social Class Segregation: Yet Another Sorting Machine?" Pp. 169–221 in *A Nation at Risk: Preserving Public Education as an Engine for Social Mobility*, edited by Richard Kahlenberg. New York: Century Foundation Press.

Wells, Amy S. et al. 1998. *Beyond the Rhetoric of Charter School Reform: A Study of Ten California Districts*. Los Angeles: University of California at Los Angeles.

West, Cornel. 1982. *The Cornel West Reader*. New York: Basic Civitas Books.

———.1993. *Race Matters*. Boston, MA: Beacon Press.

Wijnberg, M. H. and S. Weinger. 1998. "When Dreams Wither and Resources Fail: The Social Support Systems of Poor Single Mothers." *Families in Society: The Journal of Contemporary Human Services* 79: 212–19.

Wilmore, Gayraud S. (ed.). 1995. *African-American Religious Studies: An Interdisciplinary Anthology*. Durham, NC: Duke University Press.

———.1994. *Black Religion and Black Radicalism: An Interpretation of the Religious History of Afro-American People*. New York: Orbis Books.

Wilson, William Julius. 1996. *When Work Disappears: The World of the New Urban Poor*. New York: Alfred A. Knopf.

———.1987. *The Truly Disadvantaged: The Inner City, the Underclass, and Public Policy*. Chicago, IL: University of Chicago Press.

Wimberly, Anne Streaty. 1994. *Soul Stories: African American Christian Education*. Nashville, TN: Abingdon Press.

Wright, Jeremiah. 2004. "Doing Black Theology in the Black Church." Pp. 13–23 in *Living Stones in the Household of God: The Legacy and Future of Black Theology*, edited by Linda Thomas. Minneapolis, MN: Fortress Press.

Index